TEMPORA

Sources of Modern History

Quellen zur Geschichte und Politik

Texte und Quellen in Auswahl

zusammengestellt und herausgegeben
von Dr. Oliver Näpel und Dr. Rolf Theis

Ernst Klett Verlag
Stuttgart · Leipzig

Bildnachweis

Umschlag
vorn, links: f1 online digitale Bildagentur (Dieterich), Frankfurt;
vorn, Mitte: Wehrgeschichtliches Museum, Rastatt;
vorn, rechts: Corbis (RF), Düsseldorf;
hinten, links: AKG (Erich Lessing), Berlin;
hinten, Mitte: BPK, Berlin;
hinten, rechts: Helga Lade (B. Steckenreuter), Frankfurt.

S. 28: The Library of Congress (PD), Washington, D.C.;
S. 34 M1 a: Keystone, Hamburg;
S. 35 M1 d: Getty Images (Hulton Archive), München;
S. 45 M4: John Langton/R. J. Morris, Atlas of Industrializing Britain, 1780–1914, Routledge, London;
S. 46 M5: aus: Asa Briggs, Iron Bridge to Crystal Palace: Impact and Images of the Industrial Revolution, Thames and Hudson, London 1979;
S. 59 M4: Courtesy of BoondocksNet.com;
S. 69 M2: Courtesy of BoondocksNet.com;
S. 70 M3: Courtesy of BoondocksNet.com;
S. 70 M4: Courtesy of BoondocksNet.com;
S. 106: Getty Images (Hulton Archiv), München;

Nicht in allen Fällen war es uns möglich, den Rechteinhaber der Abbildungen ausfindig zu machen. Berechtigte Ansprüche werden selbstverständlich im Rahmen der üblichen Vereinbarungen abgegolten.

1. Auflage 1 6 5 4 3 2 | 2016 2015 2014 2013 2012

Alle Drucke dieser Auflage sind unverändert und können im Unterricht nebeneinander verwendet werden. Die letzten Zahlen bezeichnen jeweils die Auflage und das Jahr des Druckes.

Internetadresse: www.klett.de

Redaktion: Tobias Stankowski, Frechen
Herstellung: Krystyna Schütze
Satz: Köhler & Köhler, Taucha
Repro: Meyle + Müller, Medien-Management, Pforzheim
Druck: Medienhaus Plump, Rheinbreitenbach

Printed in Germany

ISBN: 978-3-12-430063-8

9 783124 300638

Inhalt

Introductory remarks

Dear students, and teachers

This documentary reader opens up the opportunity of learning on the basis of English language documents in the history lessons of grades 12 and 13. The reader addresses students and teachers at the many hundred schools with German-English bilingual programs. It equally addresses the innumerable classes and courses that make use of English as a working language in modular teaching sequences. It is the flexibility of bilingual modules that allows the fine-tuning of language teaching goals and content-related goals to the dispositions and abilities of the learners. There is the option of talking about English language documents in German, there is the option of having both the text analysis and the classroom discussion take place in English – and there is a wide spectrum of options in between. Even if only the English language reading competence is enhanced this is an important language teaching goal; depending on the language competence of the learners and on the percentage share of classroom communication in English, other language skills and competencies can be improved as well. In addition English language source material offers the chance of gaining a wider perspective in dealing with historical topics, thus shedding doubt on seemingly obvious and subjective ways of looking at things. From outside, from a safe distance and against the background of different traditions one may well arrive at different assessments than from documents reflecting an insider perspective.

The use of foreign language material in a content-based subject allows the systematic integration of language learning and content-related learning (=Content and Language Integrated Learning; CLIL)

The teaching experience in the bilingual classroom suggests that this integration is an important motivational factor in history lessons – but only under the premise that in history lessons there is no place for the systematic teaching of grammar. This remains the task of the English class.

Over many years it was considered self-evident that the search for English language sources for the teaching of history was the problem of each individual teacher wanting to do bilingual teaching and that this teacher would have to base his/her lessons on the source material found by systematic research and pure chance. Collaboration with like-minded colleagues did not really help enough. Now, in the age of the world-wide web, one faces exactly the opposite problem. The overabundance of materials, the sheer mass of documents and sources available, demand for a viable compilation of teaching material.

The topics covered in this volume are in line with the various state curricula for grades 12 and 13. Documentary readers provide materials in addition to the textbook used in class – to open up access to a topic, to allow for more in-depth analysis or to add additional facets. The different chapters definitely do not claim to deal with their topics exhaustively but they rather allow a glimpse at some aspects of the topic.

The source material on the American Revolution, on the Age of Imperialism and on the Cold War is predominantly in the English language, so in the German textbooks one finds them only in translation. The texts edited in this book grant direct access to these historical processes on the basis of original sources.

The chapter on the Industrial Revolution addresses the developments in Great Britain, i. e. on the historical precursor of the industrial revolutions in other countries. By focusing on the Agrarian Revolution this central facet of the Industrial Revolution is highlighted much more strongly than in German textbooks and source materials. This particular widening of the traditional German way of looking at things is achieved by the relative weighting of sub-topics.

As the chapter heading 'Perspectives' already suggests, the documents on German history between World War I and National Socialism allow a foreign perspective plus the German one - referring to the outbreak of WWI, the Treaty of Versailles and the Ruhr Crisis of 1923.
The source materials in the chapters include
- central primary sources, that might also be found in translation in German textbooks and documentary readers
- survey texts by renowned experts in the respective field
- cartoons, graphs and statistics
- examples of literary texts reflecting historical processes
- an occasional translated German document taken from an English textbook and contrasted with an English language source
- a passage from a German history textbook contrasted with a passage from a current English one.
The documents are authentic in the sense that their language has not been adapted for teaching purposes.

There is no principal difference between dealing with foreign language sources and dealing with sources in the mother tongue. But there are the additional dimensions of the problems resulting from the use of a foreign language and of the opportunities created by a widened perspective.
a. The documents are not annotated, i. e. their vocabulary is not explained. The teaching experience in bilingual classes shows that the concept of 'English as a working language' only works once the students no longer think they have to look up the translation and to precisely understand each and every single word in a text. For analyting longer and more complex documents one needs to develop strategies to minimize the use of the dictionary, for example by reconstructing the meaning of words from their context, by looking for analogies/parallels, by being aware of the rules of word formation, and by relying on the effects of redundancies. That is, only those words are to be looked up in the dictionary that are indispensable for understanding the text . It has proved rather useful for a group of learners to compile a glossary by the end of a teaching sequence and to make a list of the (functional) vocabulary learned.
Ensuring that the relevant historical terms will also be learned in German is not really a problem within the framework of bilingual modules, as in most cases only small sequences of the thematic spectrum will be dealt with in English. Normally classroom communication will mostly be in German anyway, on the basis of English language texts. Regarding lessons in the context of schools with bilingual programs it is advisable to make sure the German technical terms are also learnt - e.g. by having a backup German textbook which should be turned to especially at those points where gains from a difference in perspective are to be expected.
b. Even more so than in the normal history lesson bilingual education has to rely on students' increased awareness of methods. Longer (argumentative) documents should be analyzed step by step by the students as a group to make everybody aware of the methodical steps taken. The use of visually aided structuring of contents and line of argument is more important still than in German language document analysis; it helps to provide the basis for acquiring elements of cognitive language proficiency, e.g. the language of cohesion and words, phrases and structures expressing different kinds of logical relations.
c. Project work and independent research are key features of bilingual programs. The materials at hand can be used to serve as starting points for student inquiries and (internet) research finally leading to the presentation of results in class.
Enjoy your work in the bilingual history classroom.
Dr. Oliver Näpel
Dr. Rolf Theis

1. The American Revolution – a Milestone in History?

The American Revolution – and even more prominently its result: the Declaration of Independence – is one of the most crucial points in the history of Western civilization, at least according to many US-American historians and citizens alike. Its phrases 'unalienable rights of life, liberty, and the pursuit of happiness' as well as its program 'all men are created equal' together with the constitutional amendments, the American Bill of Rights, have been and still are a great inspiration to all people who fight for emancipation, liberty and equality from the suffragists to the various human rights organizations in the world. On the other hand, the stark contrast between the rhetorical claim and its obvious shortcomings in reality – in the United States as well as worldwide, then as well as now – has given reason for criticism of internal and external political action of the United States. As the most central founding myth the American Revolution is the main aspect of the 'American Dream' and it has been used to criticize US government as well as to legitimize their actions in the world since its inception. And although this is one of the most thoroughly studied (and publicized) aspects of US-history there is still room for debate. To what extent is the American Revolution rooted in 'European' thought? Has it been a 'revolution' at all? Is it true, that the majority of the American population during that time was either neutral or even against independence? And if this is true, why was it successful? How did the relatively small military potential of the colonies win against the British Empire? Who profited from the Revolution, who was left out and who had to 'pay the bill'? What were the political tendencies lay behind the colonist's fight for freedom? Were they egalitarian or rather elitist? The following documents may help to shed some light on these aspects, but as with many important historic events, some answers are still open for debate and will be for the foreseeable future.

1.1 Some Thoughts on the American Revolution

M1 Richard Price, 1791

Richard Price (1723–1791), Protestant minister, held a keynote address in London on 4 November 1789 for the "Society for the Commemoration of the Revolution in Great Britain" to celebrate the one hundredth anniversary of the Glorious Revolution of 1688. Here is an excerpt from Price's address:

What an eventful period this is! I am thankful that I have lived to see it; and I could almost say, Lord, now lettest thou thy servant depart in peace, for mine eyes have seen thy salvation. I have lived to see a diffusion of knowledge, which has undermined superstition and error – I have lived to see the rights of men better understood than ever; and nations panting for liberty, which seem to have lost the idea of it. I have lived to see 30 millions of people, indignant and resolute, spurning at slavery, and demanding liberty with an irresistible voice; their king led in triumph, and an arbitrary monarch surrendering himself to his subjects. – After sharing in the benefits of one revolution, I have been spared to be witness to two other revolutions, both glorious. And now methinks I see the love for liberty catching and spreading, a general amendment beginning in human affairs; the dominion of kings changed for the dominion of laws, and the dominion of priests giving way to the dominion of reason and conscience.

Be encouraged, all ye friends of freedom, and writers in its defense! The times are auspicious. Your labours have not been in vain. Behold kingdoms, admonished by you, starting from sleep, breaking their fetters, and claiming justice from their oppressors! Behold, the light you have struck out, after setting America free, reflected to France, and there kindled into a blaze that lays despotism in ashes, and warms and illuminates Europe! Tremble all ye oppressors of the world! Take warning all ye supporters of slavish governments. Take warning all ye supporters of slavish governments, and slavish hierarchies. Call no more (absurdly and wickedly) Reformation, innovation. You cannot now hold the world in darkness. Struggle no longer against increasing light and liberality. Restore to mankind their rights; and consent to the correction of abuses, before they and you are destroyed together.

Butler, Marilyn (Hrsg.): Burke, Paine, Godwin and the Revolution Controversy. Cambridge: Cambridge University Press 1984, S. 31–32.

M2 Thomas Carlyle, 1837

Thomas Carlyle (1795–1881), British essayist and historian in his famous 'The French Revolution' (3 volumes, 1837):

Alas, much more lies sick than poor Louis: not the French King only, but the French Kingship; this too, after long rough tear and wear, is breaking down. The world is all so changed; so much that seemed vigorous has sunk decrepit, so much that was not is beginning to be! Borne over the Atlantic, to the closing ear of Louis, King by the Grace of God, what sounds are these; muffled ominous, new in our centuries? Boston Harbor is black with unexpected Tea: behold a Pennsylvanian Congress gather; and ere long, on Bunker Hill, DEMOCRACY announcing, in rifle-volleys death-winged, under her Star Banner, to the tune of Yankee-doodle-doo, that she is born, and, whirlwind-like, will envelope the whole world!

Carlyle, Thomas: The French Revolution. 3 Vols., hier: Vol. I. 1837. Abgedruckt in: The World's Classics. CXXV. The Works of Thomas Carlyle. Vol. III. London (u.a.): Oxford University Press 1909, S. 9. Online: http://www.historyguide.org/intellect/lecture11a.html

M3 Gordon S. Wood

Gordon S. Wood (born 1933), Brown University, in his "The Radicalism of the American Revolution"

It was the Revolution, more than any other single event, that made America into the most liberal, democratic, and modern nation in the world.

Gordon S. Wood: The Radicalism of the American Revolution. (1992) Zitiert nach: William Dudley (Hrsg.): The American Revolution. Opposing Viewpoints. San Diego: Greenhaven Press 1992, S. 256.

M4 John F. Kennedy's Inaugural Address, 1961

Like most Presidents of the US John Fitzgerald Kennedy, who became part of the American Dream himself, albeit post-mortem, made many allusions to the founding myth of the USA in his Inaugural Address in 1961:

We observe today not a victory of party, but a celebration of freedom – symbolizing an end, as well as a beginning – signifying renewal, as well as change. For I have sworn before you and Almighty God the same solemn oath our forebears prescribed nearly a century and three-quarters ago.

The world is very different now. For man holds in his mortal hands the power to abolish all forms of human poverty and all forms of human life. And yet the same revolutionary beliefs for which our forebears fought are still at issue around the globe – the belief that the rights of man come not from the generosity of the state, but from the hand of God.

We dare not forget today that we are the heirs of that first revolution. Let the word go forth from this time and place, to friend and foe alike, that the torch has been passed to a new generation of Americans – born in this century, tempered by war, disciplined by a hard and bitter peace, proud of our ancient heritage, and unwilling to witness or permit the slow undoing of those human rights to which this nation has always been committed, and to which we are committed today at home and around the world.

Let every nation know, whether it wishes us well or ill, that we shall pay any price, bear any burden, meet any hardship, support any friend, oppose any foe, to assure the survival and the success of liberty. This much we pledge – and more. [...]

To those new states whom we welcome to the ranks of the free, we pledge our word that one form of colonial control shall not have passed away merely to be replaced by a far more iron tyranny. We shall not always expect to find them supporting our view. But we shall always hope to find them strongly supporting their own freedom – and to remember that, in the past, those who foolishly sought power by riding the back of the tiger ended up inside.

To those people in the huts and villages of half the globe struggling to break the bonds of mass misery, we pledge our best efforts to help them help themselves, for whatever period is required – not because the Communists may be doing it, not because we seek their votes, but because it is right. If a free society cannot help the many who are poor, it cannot save the few who are rich. [...]

In the long history of the world, only a few generations have been granted the role of defending freedom in its hour of maximum danger. I do not shrink from this responsibility – I welcome it. I do not believe that any of us would exchange places with any other people or any other generation. The energy, the faith, the devotion which we bring to this endeavor will light our country and all who serve it. And the glow from that fire can truly light the world. And so, my fellow Americans, ask not what your country can do for you; ask what you can do for your country. My fellow citizens of the world, ask not what America will do for you, but what together we can do for the freedom of man.

http://www.americanrhetoric.com/speeches/jfkinaugural.htm

M5 Independence Day

As this movie is still easily available on DVD and as this scene is rather 'simple' but nevertheless effective, enforced by easy to decode cinematic devices, it can be used perfectly in the history classroom in the context of media literacy as well as as an example of contemporary use of history and historical allusions in popular media.

The fictitious President, Thomas Whitmore, holds a speech on the eve of the final battle versus the alien invaders to lighten up the spirit of the soldiers.

Good Morning.

In less than an hour aircraft from here will join others from around the world. And you will be launching the largest aerial battle in the history of Mankind.

Mankind – that word should have new meaning for all of us today. We can't be consumed in our petty differences anymore. We will be united by our common interest. Perhaps it is fate that today is the fourth of July and you will once again be fighting for our freedom. Not from tyranny, oppression, or persecution, but from annihilation. We're fighting for our right to live, to exist! And should we win the day, the 4th of July will no longer be known as an American holiday, but as the day when the world declared in one voice, "We will not go quietly into the night! We will not vanish without a fight! We're going to live on! We're going to survive! Today, we celebrate our Independence Day!

Independence Day; Roland Emmerich (dir.), Twentieth Century Fox Film Corporation, 1996; Transkript O. Näpel.

M6 Independence Day Speech by President Bush, 2006

President George W. Bush thanks Military on Independence Day at Fort Bragg, North Carolina, in 2006.

Today we mark the 230th anniversary of American independence. And on this day, when we give thanks for our freedom, we also give thanks for the men and women who make our freedom possible. Each of you have stepped forward to serve, knowing the risks and dangers that accompany freedom's defense.

I've come to thank you for your valor, and to thank you for your patriotism. I've come to share with you, and with the American people, how your dedication and your sacrifice are helping us win the war on terror. (*Ap-*

plause.) You are serving our country at a time when our country needs you. And because of your courage, every day is Independence Day in America. (*Applause.*) [...]

Two-hundred-and-thirty years ago, 56 brave men signed their names to a document that set the course of our nation. It changed the history of the world. Our Declaration of Independence was a bold statement of revolutionary principles. It laid down a creed of freedom and a quality that has lifted the lives of hundreds of millions here in America and around the world. Yet, without the courage of the soldiers of our Continental Army, the words of the Declaration would have been forgotten by history, dismissed as the radical musings of a failed revolution.

We celebrate Independence Day each year because that ragtag group of citizen soldiers challenged the world's most powerful military, secured our liberty and planted a standard of freedom to which the entire world has aspired.

Since that first 4th of July, some 43 million Americans have defended our freedom in times of war. These brave men and women crossed oceans and continents to defeat murderous ideologies and to secure the peace for generations that followed. We live in liberty because of the courage they displayed – from Bunker Hill to Baghdad, from Concord to Kabul – on this Independence Day we honor their achievements and we thank them for their service in freedom's cause. (*Applause.*) [...]

There's more work to be done in Iraq. The Iraqi people face deadly enemies who are determined to stop Iraq's new unity government from succeeding. They can't stand the thought of liberty. [...]

By achieving victory in Iraq, we will help Iraqis build a free nation in the heart of a troubled region, and inspire those who desire liberty – those democratic reformers from Damascus to Teheran. By achieving victory in Iraq, we will honor the sacrifice of the brave men and women who have risked their lives and given their lives for a just and noble cause. [...]

You've given our citizens a priceless gift, the opportunity to live in freedom and to pursue their dreams, and enjoy lives of purpose and dignity. You've kept America what our founders meant her to be: a light to the nations, spreading the good news of human freedom to the darkest corners of earth.

I want to thank you for all you do for our country and for the world. May God bless you all, and may God continue to bless the United States of America. (*Applause.*)

http://www.whitehouse.gov/news/releases/2006/07/20060704.html

M7 Excerpts from the Magna Carta, 1215

John, by the grace of God King of England, Lord of Ireland, Duke of Normandy and Aquitaine, and Count of Anjou, to his archbishops, bishops, abbots, earls, barons, justices, foresters, sheriffs, stewards, servants, and to all his officials and loyal subjects, Greeting. [...]

[1] First, that we have granted to God, and by this present charter have confirmed for us and our heirs in perpetuity, that the English Church shall be free, and shall have its rights undiminished, and its liberties unimpaired. That we wish this so to be observed, appears from the fact that of our own free will, before the outbreak of the present dispute between us and our barons, we granted and confirmed by charter the freedom of the Church's elections – a right reckoned to be of the greatest necessity and importance to it – and caused this to be confirmed by Pope Innocent III. This freedom we shall observe ourselves, and desire to be observed in good faith by our heirs in perpetuity.

To all free men of our kingdom we have also granted, for us and our heirs for ever, all the liberties written out below, to have and to keep for them and their heirs, of us and our heirs: [...]

[12] No 'scutage' [e.g. cash payment instead of performing the knightly military duties] or 'aid' of money paid instead of may be levied in our kingdom without its general consent, unless it is for the ransom of our person, to make our eldest son a knight, and (once) to marry our eldest daughter. For these pur-

poses only a reasonable 'aid' may be levied. 'Aids' from the city of London are to be treated similarly.

[13] The city of London shall enjoy all its ancient liberties and free customs, both by land and by water. We also will and grant that all other cities, boroughs, towns, and ports shall enjoy all their liberties and free customs.

[14] To obtain the general consent of the realm for the assessment of an 'aid' – except in the three cases specified above – or a 'scutage', we will cause the archbishops, bishops, abbots, earls, and greater barons to be summoned individually by letter. To those who hold lands directly of us we will cause a general summons to be issued, through the sheriffs and other officials, to come together on a fixed day (of which at least forty days notice shall be given) and at a fixed place. [...]

[39] No free man shall be seized or imprisoned, or stripped of his rights or possessions, or outlawed or exiled, or deprived of his standing in any other way, nor will we proceed with force against him, or send others to do so, except by the lawful judgement of his equals or by the law of the land.

[40] To no one will we sell, to no one deny or delay right or justice.

[42] In future it shall be lawful for any man to leave and return to our kingdom unharmed and without fear, by land or water, preserving his allegiance to us, except in time of war, for some short period, for the common benefit of the realm. People that have been imprisoned or outlawed in accordance with the law of the land, people from a country that is at war with us, and merchants – who shall be dealt with as stated above – are excepted from this provision. [...]

Douglas, David C. (Hrsg.): English Historical Documents. 12 Bände. London: Eyre & Spottiswoode 1955–1975. Volume III (hrsgg. von Harry Rothwell), 1975, S. 316–323.

M8 Mayflower Compact

Prior to their landing at Plymouth Rock in 1620 forty-one passengers, all of them Puritans, signed a document that came to be known as the Mayflower Compact, named after the ship the travelers arrived on. It was meant to prevent dissent and the dissolution of the group after their landing and became the foundation of Plymouth's government.

In the name of God, Amen. We, whose names are underwritten, the Loyal Subjects of our dread Sovereign Lord, King James, by the Grace of God, of England, France and Ireland, King, Defender of the Faith, e&. Having undertaken for the Glory of God, and Advancement of the Christian Faith, and the Honour of our King and Country, a voyage to plant the first colony in the northern parts of Virginia; do by these present, solemnly and mutually in the Presence of God and one of another, covenant and combine ourselves together into a civil Body Politick, for our better Ordering and Preservation, and Furtherance of the Ends aforesaid; And by Virtue hereof to enact, constitute, and frame, such just and equal Laws, Ordinances, Acts, Constitutions and Offices, from time to time, as shall be thought most meet and convenient for the General good of the Colony; unto which we promise all due submission and obedience. In Witness whereof we have hereunto subscribed our names at Cape Cod the eleventh of November, in the Reign of our Sovereign Lord, King James of *England, France and Ireland, the eighteenth, and of Scotland the fifty-fourth. Anno Domini, 1620.*

Morison, Samuel Eliot (Hrsg.): William Bradford, Of Plymouth Plantation, 1620–1647. New York: 1991, S. 75–76. Online: http://usinfo.state.gov/usa/infousa/facts/democrac/2.htm

M9 Encyclopaedia Britannica: Bill of Rights

Formally *An Act Declaring the Rights and Liberties of the Subject and Settling the Succession of the Crown* (1689) one of the basic instruments of the British constitution, the result of the long 17th-century struggle between the Stuart kings and the English people and Parliament.. [...] With the Toleration Act (1689), granting religious toleration to all Protestants, the Triennial Act (1694), ordering general elections to be held every three years, and the Act of Settlement (1701) [...], the Bill of Rights provided the foundation on

which the government rested after the Glorious Revolution (1688–89). It purported to introduce no new principles but merely to declare explicitly the existing law. The revolution settlement, however, made monarchy clearly conditional on the will of Parliament and provided a freedom from arbitrary government of which most Englishmen were notably proud during the 18th century.
The main purpose of the act was unequivocally to declare illegal various practices of James II. Among such practices proscribed were the royal prerogative of dispensing with the law in certain cases, the complete suspension of laws without the consent of Parliament, and the levying of taxes and the maintenance of a standing army in peacetime without specific parliamentary authorization. A number of clauses sought to eliminate royal interference in parliamentary matters, stressing that elections must be free and that members must have complete freedom of speech. Certain forms of interference in the course of justice were also proscribed. [...]

"Bill of Rights." Encyclopædia Britannica from Encyclopædia Britannica 2007 Ultimate Reference Suite. (2007).

M10 Bill of Rights

An Act Declaring the Rights and Liberties of the Subject and Settling the Succession of the Crown (1689)

[...] And thereupon the said Lords Spiritual and Temporal and Commons, pursuant to their respective letters and elections, being now assembled in a full and free representative of this nation, taking into their most serious consideration the best means for attaining the ends aforesaid, do in the first place (as their ancestors in like case have usually done) for the vindicating and asserting their ancient rights and liberties declare;
That the pretended power of suspending the laws or the execution of laws by regal authority without consent of Parliament is illegal;
That levying money for or to the use of the Crown by pretence of prerogative, without grant of Parliament, for longer time, or in other manner than the same is or shall be granted, is illegal; [...]
That the raising or keeping a standing army within the kingdom in time of peace, unless it be with consent of Parliament, is against law;
That the subjects which are Protestants may have arms for their defence suitable to their conditions and as allowed by law;
That election of members of Parliament ought to be free;
And that for redress of all grievances, and for the amending, strengthening and preserving of the laws, Parliaments ought to be held frequently. [...]

Douglas, David C. (Hrsg.): English Historical Documents. 12 Bände. London: Eyre & Spottiswoode 1955–1975. Volume VIII (hrsgg. von Andrew Browning), 1966, S. 122–128. Online: http://www.yale.edu/lawweb/avalon/england.htm

1.2 The Beginning of the Conflict

1.2.1 Stamp Act

The British Parliament tried to raise revenue through direct taxation of the colonies in order to help ease the financial burden of the French and Indian War (1756–1763) that had taken place in Northern America – a common means of consolidating the national budget. The heated opposition in the colonies and among English people in the motherland who sympathized with the Americans' point of view led to three major 'legal conflicts', namely the discussions about the Sugar Act (1764), the Stamp Act (1765) and the Declaratory Act (1765).

M1 Resolutions of the Stamp Act Congress

In order to coordinate possible action against the Stamp Act a Congress was called into life. Several colonies sent delegations to this Congress in New York in the summer of 1765.

The members of this Congress, sincerely devoted, with the warmest sentiments of affection and duty to His Majesty's Person and Government, inviolably attached to the present happy establishment of the Protestant succession, and with minds deeply impressed by a sense of the present and impending misfortunes of the British colonies on this continent; having considered as maturely as time will permit the circumstances of the said colonies, esteem it our indispensable duty to make the following declarations of our humble opinion, respecting the most essential rights and liberties of the colonists, and of the grievances under which they labour, by reason of several late Acts of Parliament.

That His Majesty's subjects in these colonies, owe the same allegiance to the Crown of Great-Britain, that is owing from his subjects born within the realm, and all due subordination to that august body the Parliament of Great-Britain.

That His Majesty's liege subjects in these colonies, are entitled to all the inherent rights and liberties of his natural born subjects within the kingdom of Great-Britain.

That it is inseparably essential to the freedom of a people, and the undoubted right of Englishmen, that no taxes be imposed on them, but with their own consent, given personally, or by their representatives.

That the people of these colonies are not, and from their local circumstances cannot be, represented in the House of Commons in Great-Britain.

That the only representatives of the people of these colonies, are persons chosen therein by themselves, and that no taxes ever have been, or can be constitutionally imposed on them, but by their respective legislatures.

That all supplies to the Crown, being free gifts of the people, it is unreasonable and inconsistent with the principles and spirit of the British Constitution, for the people of Great-Britain to grant to His Majesty the property of the colonists.

That trial by jury is the inherent and invaluable right of every British subject in these colonies.

That the late Act of Parliament, entitled, An Act for granting and applying certain Stamp Duties, and other Duties, in the British colonies and plantations in America, etc., by imposing taxes on the inhabitants of these colonies, and the said Act, and several other Acts, by extending the jurisdiction of the courts of Admiralty beyond its ancient limits, have a manifest tendency to subvert the rights and liberties of the colonists.

That the duties imposed by several late Acts of Parliament, from the peculiar circumstances of these colonies, will be extremely burthensome and grievous; and from the scarcity of specie, the payment of them absolutely impracticable.

That as the profits of the trade of these colonies ultimately center in Great-Britain, to pay for the manufactures which they are obliged to take from thence, they eventually contribute very largely to all supplies granted there to the Crown.

That the restrictions imposed by several late Acts of Parliament, on the trade of these colonies, will render them unable to purchase the manufactures of Great-Britain.

That the increase, prosperity, and happiness of these colonies, depend on the full and free enjoyment of their rights and liberties, and an intercourse with Great-Britain mutually affectionate and advantageous.

Douglas, David C. (Hrsg.): English Historical Documents. 12 Bände. London: Eyre & Spottiswoode 1955–1975. Volume IX (hrsgg. von Harry Rothwell) 1969, S. 672 f.

M2 An Act Repealing the Stamp Act; March 18, 1766

The Stamp Act was repealed despite many opposing voices in the House of Lords and mainly as the result of a flood of petitions by British merchants whose products had been boycotted in the colonies.

Whereas an Act was passed in the last session of Parliament entitled An Act for Granting and

Applying Certain Stamp Duties, and Other Duties in the British Colonies and Plantations in America Towards Further Defraying the Expenses of Defending, Protecting, and Securing the Same; and for amending such parts of the several Acts of Parliament relating to the trade and revenues of the said colonies and plantations as direct the manner of determining and recovering the penalties and forfeitures therein mentioned; and whereas the continuance of the said Act would be attended with many inconveniencies, and may be productive of consequences greatly detrimental to the commercial interests of these kingdoms; may it therefore please your most excellent Majesty that it may be enacted; and be it enacted by the king's most excellent Majesty, by and with the advice and consent of the Lords Spiritual and Temporal, and Commons, in this present Parliament assembled, and by the authority of the same, that from and after the first day of May, one thousand seven hundred and sixty-six, the above-mentioned Act, and the several matters and things therein contained, shall be, and is and are hereby repealed and made void to all intents and purposes whatsoever.

Douglas, David C. (Hrsg.): English Historical Documents. 12 Bände. London: Eyre & Spottiswoode 1955–1975. Volume IX (hrsgg. von Harry Rothwell) 1969, S. 695.

M3 Declaratory Act

The repeal of the Stamp Act was 'flanked' by the following Act:

An Act for the Better Securing the Dependency of His Majesty's Dominions in America upon the Crown and Parliament of Great Britain

Whereas several of the houses of representatives in His Majesty's colonies and plantations in America have of late, against law, claimed to themselves, or to the general assemblies of the same, the sole and exclusive right of imposing duties and taxes upon His Majesty's subjects in the said colonies and plantations; and have, in pursuance of such claim, passed certain votes, resolutions, and orders derogatory to the legislative authority of Parliament, and inconsistent with the dependency of the said colonies and plantations upon the crown of Great Britain: may it therefore please Your Most Excellent Majesty that it may be declared, and be it declared by the king's Most Excellent Majesty, by and with the advice and consent of the Lords Spiritual and Temporal, and Commons, in this present Parliament assembled, and by the authority of the same, that the said colonies and plantations in America have been, are, and of right ought to be, subordinate unto, and dependent upon the imperial crown and Parliament of Great Britain; and that the king's Majesty, by and with the advice and consent of the Lords Spiritual and Temporal, and Commons, of Great Britain, in Parliament assembled, had, hath, and of right ought to have, full power and authority to make laws and statutes of sufficient force and validity to bind the colonies and people of America, subjects of the crown of Great Britain, in all cases whatsoever. [...]

And be it further declared and enacted by the authority aforesaid, that all resolutions, votes, orders, and proceedings, in any of the said colonies or plantations, whereby the power and authority of the Parliament of Great Britain to make laws and statutes as aforesaid is denied, or drawn into question, are, and are hereby declared to be, utterly null and void to all intents and purposes whatsoever.

Douglas, David C. (Hrsg.): English Historical Documents. 12 Bände. London: Eyre & Spottiswoode 1955–1975. Volume IX (hrsg. von Harry Rothwell) 1969, S. 695 f.

1.3 Escalation of the Conflict

1.3.1 Townshend Acts and the Boston Tea Party

Needing to balance the national budget, English Parliament passed four acts in 1767 named after the chancellor of the Exchequer, Charles Townshend (1725 – 1767), time to whose initiative these acts can be attributed. Using the difference between internal and external taxation one act raised an import tax on various goods brought to the colonies, such as lead, glass and tea. Although not a directed tax, together with the other acts that led to an increase in the number of British troops in the colonies, and allowed for dissolution of local government, these acts intensified the hostility between colonists and British troops, hostility that erupted in the infamous Boston Massacre in 1770. After the repeal of the Townshend Acts in 1770 the English Parliament issued a Tea Act in 1773 in order to allow the East India Company to become competitive enough to sell its vast amount of tea stored in England. The colonists again perceived this as undue interference in 'colonial affairs' which again led to hostilities and counter-measures by the colonists, e.g. the famous Boston Tea Party, when colonists masquerading as Indians destroyed three shipments of tea belonging to the East India Company by throwing it into Boston harbour. Not all colonists were in favor of such drastic measures.

M1 A Loyalist's Point of View

On 7 December 1773, the residents of Plymouth, Massachusetts, passed a set of strong resolutions against the Tea Act, an attempt by the British to ship and sell, with tax, tea to the colonies. One week later some residents of the town, fearing reprisal from the British, attempted to have the resolutions reconsidered. When they failed, they published the following protest on 23 December 1773, in the Massachusetts Gazette:

That it is not only our right but our duty frankly and freely to express our sentiments on every matter which essentially concerns the safety and welfare of our country, is a trust which we apprehend cannot be denied.

Therefore, We who are inhabitants of the town of Plymouth neither captivated by sounds and declamations, nor deceived by the cunning stratagems of men who under the specious masque of patriotism have attempted to delude an innocent and loyal people; but firmly and steadily fix'd and determin'd to defend our rights and privileges, and to endeavour to hand to our posterity the blessings of peace and good government which were procured by our fathers and transmitted to US, – Having taken into serious consideration the dangerous and fatal consequences which may arise from the late resolves pass'd at a meeting of this town […]; Fearing that they may bring upon us the vengeance of affronted Majesty and his insulted authority, We cannot answer it to our God and our consciences unless we protest against the proceedings of said meetings, and publish to the world that we were not instrumental in procuring those mischiefs which may naturally be expected from such conduct. – And we do by these presents solemnly protest against the whole of said resolves as being repugnant to our ideas of Liberty, law and reason. […]

William Dudley (Hrsg.): The American Revolution. Opposing Viewpoints. San Diego: Greenhaven Press 1992, S. 93 f.

30

1.4 Independence

M1 The First Continental Congress: The Declaration of Colonial Rights and Grievances, 1 October 1774

As a response to the Parliament's Coercive (or: Intolerable) Act in 1774, which in itself had been a response to various acts of colonial defiance, not least the Boston Tea Party (1773), the (first) Continental Congress convened in Philadelphia to discuss possible counter measures. It drew a resolution in order to achieve the repeal of the Coercive Acts which turned out to be very much a forerunner of the Declaration of Independence, both in form and content.

Whereas, since the close of the last war, the British parliament, claiming a power of right to bind the people of America by statute in all cases whatsoever, hath, in some acts expressly imposed taxes on them, and in others, under various pretenses, but in fact for the purpose of raising a revenue, hath imposed rates and duties payable in these colonies, established a board of commissioners with unconstitutional powers, and extended the jurisdiction of courts of Admiralty not only for collecting the said duties, but for the trial of causes merely arising within the body of a county.

And whereas, in consequence of other statutes, judges who before held only estates at will in their offices, have been made dependent on the Crown alone for their salaries, and standing armies kept in times of peace.

And it has lately been resolved in Parliament, that by force of a statute made in the thirty-fifth year of the reign of king Henry the Eighth, colonists may be transported to England, and tried there upon accusations for treasons. [...]

And whereas, in the last session of Parliament, three statutes were made; [...] All which statutes are impolitic, unjust, and cruel, as well as unconstitutional, and most dangerous and destructive of American rights.

And whereas, Assemblies have been frequently dissolved, contrary to the rights of the people, when they attempted to deliberate on grievances; and their dutiful, humble, loyal, & reasonable petitions to the crown for redress, have been repeatedly treated with contempt, by His Majesty's ministers of state:

The good people of the several Colonies of New Hampshire, Massachusetts bay, Rhode Island and Providence plantations, Connecticut, New York, New Jersey, Pennsylvania, Newcastle Kent and Sussex on Delaware, Maryland, Virginia, North Carolina, and South Carolina, justly alarmed at these arbitrary proceedings of Parliament and administration, have severally elected, constituted, and appointed deputies to meet, and sit in general Congress, in the city of Philadelphia, in order to obtain such establishment, as that their religion, laws, and liberties, may not be subverted:

Whereupon the deputies so appointed being now assembled, [...] declare,

- That the inhabitants of the English Colonies in North America, by the immutable laws of nature, the principles of the English constitution, and the several charters or compacts, have the following Rights: [...]
- That the foundation of English liberty, and of all free government, is a right in the people to participate in their legislative council: and as the English colonists are not represented, and from their local and other circumstances, cannot properly be represented in the British parliament, they are entitled to a free and exclusive power of legislation in their several provincial legislatures, where their right of representation can alone be preserved, in all cases of taxation and internal polity, subject only to the negative of their sovereign, in such manner as has been heretofore used and accustomed. [...]
- That the respective colonies are entitled to the common law of England, and more especially to the great and inestimable privilege of being tried by their peers of the vicinage, according to the course of that law. [...]
- That they have a right peaceably to assemble, consider of their grievances, and petition the King; and that all prosecutions, pro-

hibitory proclamations, and commitments for the same, are illegal.

• That the keeping a Standing army in these colonies, in times of peace, without the consent of the legislature of that colony in which such army is kept, is against law. [...]

All and each of which the aforesaid deputies, in behalf of themselves, and their constituents, do claim, demand, and insist on, as their indubitable rights and liberties; which cannot be legally taken from them, altered or abridged by any power whatever, without their own consent, by their representatives in their several provincial legislatures.

In the course of our inquiry, we find many infringements and violations of the foregoing rights, which, from an ardent desire that harmony and mutual intercourse of affection and interest may be restored, we pass over for the present, and proceed to state such acts and measures as have been adopted since the last war, which demonstrate a system formed to enslave America.

[...] To these grievous acts and measures Americans cannot submit, but in hopes that their fellow subjects in Great Britain will, on a revision of them, restore us to that state in which both countries found happiness and prosperity, we have for the present only resolved to pursue the following peaceable measures: 1st. To enter into a non-importation, non-consumption, and non-exportation agreement or association. 2. To prepare an address to the people of Great Britain, and a memorial to the inhabitants of British America, & 3. To prepare a loyal address to his Majesty, agreeable to resolutions already entered into.

Douglas, David C. (Hrsg.): English Historical Documents. 12 Bände. London: Eyre & Spottiswoode 1955–1975. Volume IX (hrsgg. von Harry Rothwell) 1969, S. 805–808.

M2 Patrick Henry: Give Me Liberty

Patrick Henry (1736–1799) was part of the radical opposition to the British government and a prominent figure in the American Revolution, e.g. a member of the Continental Congress. As it became more and more obvious that the clash with the English government would turn into a military conflict the colonies convened to decide whether to participate in such military actions against England. In 1775 Henry is believed to have held a speech at the second Virginia Convention, the last line of which became very famous later. The fact, that there is no contemporary recording of this and that the first public record of it appears only in a biographer's work (William Wirt) some 40 years later has given rise to doubtson whether this speech was truly held as reported (see http://ask.metafilter.com/19818/Did-Patrick-Henry-ever-do-anything-hes-credited-with). Anyhow this speech has taken root in the founding myths of the US.

No man thinks more highly than I do of the patriotism, as well as abilities, of the very worthy gentlemen who have just addressed the House. But different men often see the same subject in different lights; and, therefore, I hope that it will not be thought disrespectful to those gentlemen, if, [...] I shall speak forth my sentiments freely and without reserve.

This is no time for ceremony. The question before the House is one of awful moment to this country. For my own part I consider it as nothing less than a question of freedom or slavery; and in proportion to the magnitude of the subject ought to be the freedom of the debate. [...]

Mr. President, it is natural to man to indulge in the illusions of hope. We are apt to shut our eyes against a painful truth, and listen to the song of that siren, till she transforms us into beasts. Is this the part of wise men, engaged in a great and arduous struggle for liberty? Are we disposed to be of the number of those who, having eyes, see not, and having ears, hear not, the things which so nearly concern their temporal salvation?

For my part, whatever anguish of spirit it may cost, I am willing to know the whole truth – to know the worst and to provide for it. I have but one lamp by which my feet are guided; and that is the lamp of experience. I know of no way of judging of the future but by the past. And judging by the past, I wish to know what there has been in the conduct of the British ministry for the last ten years, to justify those hopes with which gentlemen have been pleased to solace themselves and the House? Is it that insidious smile with which our petition has been lately received? Trust it not, sir; it will prove a snare to your feet. Suffer not yourselves to be betrayed with a kiss. Ask yourselves how this gracious reception of our petition comports with these warlike preparations which cover our waters and darken our land. Are fleets and armies necessary to a work of love and reconciliation? Have we shown ourselves so unwilling to be reconciled that force must be called in to win back our love? Let us not deceive ourselves, sir. These are the implements of war and subjugation – the last arguments to which kings resort. I ask gentlemen, sir, what means this martial array, if its purpose be not to force us to submission?

[…] And what have we to oppose to them? Shall we try argument? Sir, we have been trying that for the last ten years. Have we anything new to offer on the subject? Nothing. […]

Sir, we have done everything that could be done to avert the storm which is now coming on. We have petitioned; we have remonstrated; we have supplicated; we have prostrated ourselves before the throne, and have implored its interposition to arrest the tyrannical hands of the ministry and Parliament.

Our petitions have been slighted; our remonstrances have produced additional violence and insult; our supplications have been disregarded; and we have been spurned, with contempt, from the foot of the throne. In vain, after these things, may we indulge the fond hope of peace and reconciliation. There is no longer any room for hope.

If we wish to be free – if we mean to preserve inviolate those inestimable privileges for which we have been so long contending – if we mean not basely to abandon the noble struggle in which we have been so long engaged, and which we have pledged ourselves never to abandon until the glorious object of our contest shall be obtained, we must fight! I repeat it, sir, we must fight! An appeal to arms and to the God of Hosts is all that is left us!

[…] Sir, we are not weak, if we make a proper use of the means which the God of nature hath placed in our power. Three millions of people, armed in the holy cause of liberty, and in such a country as that which we possess, are invincible by any force which our enemy can send against us. Besides, sir, we shall not fight our battles alone. There is a just God who presides over the destinies of nations, and who will raise up friends to fight our battles for us.

The battle, sir, is not to the strong alone; it is to the vigilant, the active, the brave. Besides, sir, we have no election. If we were base enough to desire it, it is now too late to retire from the contest. There is no retreat but in submission and slavery! Our chains are forged! Their clanking may be heard on the plains of Boston! The war is inevitable – and let it come! I repeat it, sir, let it come!

It is in vain, sir, to extenuate the matter. Gentlemen may cry, "Peace! Peace!" – but there is no peace. The war is actually begun! The next gale that sweeps from the north will bring to our ears the clash of resounding arms! Our brethren are already in the field! Why stand we here idle? What is it that gentlemen wish? What would they have? Is life so dear, or peace so sweet, as to be purchased at the price of chains and slavery? Forbid it, Almighty God! I know not what course others may take; but as for me, give me liberty, or give me death!

Wirt, William: Sketches of the Life and Character of Patrick Henry. Philadelphia: Webster 1817.
Online: http://www.historyplace.com/speeches/henry.htm

M3 Declaration of Independence

The Unanimous Declaration of the Thirteen United States of America, Juli 4, 1776

When, in the Course of human Events, it becomes necessary for one People to dissolve the Political Bands which have connected them with another, and to assume, among the Powers of the Earth, the separate and equal

Station to which the Laws of Nature and of Nature's God entitle them, a decent Respect to the Opinions of Mankind requires that they should declare the Causes which impel them to the Separation.

We hold these Truths to be self-evident, that all Men are created equal, that they are endowed, by their Creator, with certain unalienable Rights, that among these are Life, Liberty, and the Pursuit of Happiness. – That to secure these Rights, Governments are instituted among Men, deriving their just Powers from the Consent of the Governed, that whenever any Form of Government becomes destructive of these Ends, it is the Right of the People to alter or to abolish it, and to institute new Government, laying its Foundation on such Principles, and organizing its Powers in such Form, as to them shall seem most likely to effect their Safety and Happiness. Prudence, indeed, will dictate, that Governments long established, should not be changed for light and transient Causes; and accordingly all Experience hath shewn, that Mankind are more disposed to suffer, while Evils are sufferable, than to right themselves by abolishing the Forms to which they are accustomed. But when a long Train of Abuses and Usurpations, pursuing invariably the same Object, evinces a Design to reduce them under absolute Despotism, it is their Right, it is their Duty, to throw off such Government, and to provide new Guards for their future Security. Such has been the patient Sufferance of these Colonies; and such is now the Necessity which constrains them to alter their former Systems of Government. The History of the present King of Great-Britain is a History of repeated Injuries and Usurpations, all having in direct Object the Establishment of an absolute Tyranny over these States. To prove this, let Facts be submitted to a candid World.

HE has refused his Assent to Laws, the most wholesome and necessary for the public Good. [...] HE has erected a Multitude of new Offices, and sent hither Swarms of Officers to harrass our People, and eat out their Substance. HE has kept among us, in Times of Peace, Standing Armies, without the Consent of our Legislatures. [...]

FOR quartering large Bodies of Armed Troops among us: FOR protecting them, by a mock Trial, from Punishment for any Murders which they should commit on the Inhabitants of these States: [...] FOR imposing Taxes on us without our Consent: FOR depriving us, in many Cases, of the Benefits of Trial by Jury: FOR taking away our Charters, abolishing our most valuable Laws, and altering fundamentally the Forms of our Governments: [...]

HE is, at this Time, transporting large Armies of foreign Mercenaries to complete the Works of Death, Desolation, and Tyranny, already begun with Circumstances of Cruelty and Perfidy, scarcely paralleled in the most barbarous Ages, and totally unworthy the Head of a civilized Nation.

HE has constrained our Fellow-Citizens, taken Captive on the high Seas, to bear Arms against their Country, to become the Executioners of their Friends and Brethren, or to fall themselves by their Hands.

HE has excited domestic Insurrections amongst us, and has endeavoured to bring on the Inhabitants of our Frontiers, the merciless Indian Savages, whose known Rule of Warfare, is an undistinguished Destruction, of all Ages, Sexes, and Conditions.

In every Stage of these Oppressions we have Petitioned for Redress in the most humble Terms: Our repeated Petitions have been answered only by repeated Injury. A Prince, whose Character is thus marked by every Act which may define a Tyrant, is unfit to be the Ruler of a free People.

Nor have we been wanting in Attentions to our British Brethren. We have warned them, from Time to Time, of Attempts by their Legislature to extend an unwarrantable Jurisdiction over us. We have reminded them of the Circumstances of our Emigration and Settlement here. We have appealed to their native Justice and Magnanimity, and we have conjured them by the Ties of our common Kindred to disavow these Usurpations, which would inevitably interrupt our Connexions

and Correspondence. They too have been deaf to the Voice of Justice and of Consanguinity. We must, therefore, acquiesce in the Necessity, which denounces our Separation, and hold them, as we hold the Rest of Mankind, Enemies in War, in Peace Friends.
WE, therefore, the Representatives of the United States of America, in General Congress Assembled, appealing to the Supreme Judge of the World for the Rectitude of our Intentions, do, in the Name, and by Authority of the good People of these Colonies, solemnly Publish and Declare, That these United Colonies are, and of Right ought to be, Free and Independent States; that they are absolved from all Allegiance to the British Crown, and that all political Connexion between them and the State of Great-Britain, is, and ought to be, totally dissolved; and that as Free and Independent States, they have full Power to levy War, conclude Peace, contract Alliances, establish Commerce, and to do all other Acts and Things which Independent States may of Right do. And for the Support of this Declaration, with a firm Reliance on the Protection of Divine Providence, we mutually pledge to each other our Lives, our Fortunes, and our sacred Honour.

Douglas, David C. (Hrsg.): English Historical Documents. 12 Bände. London: Eyre & Spottiswoode 1955–1975. Volume IX (hrsgg. von Harry Rothwell) 1969, S. 878–880. Online: http://www.loc.gov/rr/program/bib/ourdocs/DeclarInd.html

M4 Discussion about Political Participation

a) Samuel Adams: Natural Rights Should Form the Basis of Government 1772

Samuel Adams was an American political leader whose writings and speeches helped instigate the drive for American independence. Highlights of his political career include membership in the Continental Congress and the signing of the Declaration of Independence.

Among the natural rights of the colonists are these: first, a right to life; second, to liberty; third, to property; together with the right to support and defend them in the best manner they can. These are evident branches of, rather than deductions from, the duty of self-preservation, commonly called the first law of nature. [...]
All men have a right to remain in a state of nature as long as they please; in case of intolerable oppression, civil or religious, to leave the society they belong to, and enter into another.
When men enter into society, it is by voluntary consent; and they have a right to demand and insist upon the performance of such conditions and previous limitations as from an equitable original compact. [...]
"Just and true liberty, equal and impartial liberty," in matters spiritual and temporal, is a thing that all men are clearly entitled to by the eternal and immutable laws of God and nature, as well as by the law of nations [...]
The natural liberty of man, by entering into society, is abridged or restrained so far only as is necessary for the great end of society, the best good of the whole.

William Dudley (Hrsg.): The American Revolution. Opposing Viewpoints. San Diego: Greenhaven Press 1992, S. 197–201.

b) Who Should Vote? Letter from John Adams to James Sullivan, May 26, 1776

John Adams reveals some of his ideas about the limits to direct democracy in a letter to James Sullivan, a Massachusetts legislator, who had made some suggestions about altering the legal qualifications for voters.

It is certain in theory, that the only moral foundation of government is the consent of the people. But to what an extent shall we carry this principle? Shall we say, that every individual of the community, old and young, male and female, as well as rich and poor, must consent, expressly, to every act of legislation? No, you will say. This is impossible. How then does the right arise in the majority to govern the minority, against their will? Whence arises the right of the men to govern women, without their consent? Whence the right of the old to bind the young, without theirs?
But let us first suppose, that the whole community of every age, rank, sex, and condition, has a right to vote. This community, is assem-

bled – a motion is made and carried by a majority of one voice. The minority will not agree to this. Whence arises the right of the majority to govern, and the obligation of the minority to obey? From necessity, you will say, because there can be no other rule. But why exclude women? You will say, because their delicacy renders them unfit for practice and experience, in the great business of life, and the hardy enterprises of war, as well as the arduous cares of state. Besides, their attention is so much engaged with the necessary nurture of their children, that nature has made them fittest for domestic cares. And children have not judgment or will of their own. True. But will not these reasons apply to others? Is it not equally true, that men in general in every society, who are wholly destitute of property, are also too little acquainted with public affairs to form a right judgment, and too dependent upon other men to have a will of their own? If this is a fact, if you give to every man, who has no property, a vote, will you not make a fine encouraging provision for corruption by your fundamental law? Such is the frailty of the human heart, that very few men, who have no property, have any judgment of their own. They talk and vote as they are directed by some man of property, who has attached their minds to his interest [...]

I should think that wisdom and policy would dictate in these times, to be very cautious of making alterations. Our people have never been very rigid in scrutinizing into the qualifications of voters, and I presume they will not now begin to be so. But I would not advise them to make any alteration in the laws, at present, respecting the qualifications of voters.

Your idea, that those laws, which affect the lives and personal liberty of all, or which inflict corporal punishment, affect those, who are not qualified to vote, as well as those who are, is just. But, so they do women, as well as men, children as well as adults. What reason should there be, for excluding a man of twenty years, Eleven months and twenty-seven days old, from a vote when you admit one, who is twenty one? The reason is, you must fix upon some period in life, when the understanding and will of men in general is fit to be trusted by the public. Will not the same reason justify the state in fixing upon some certain quantity of property, as a qualification. [...]

Society can be governed only by general rules. Government cannot accommodate itself to every particular case, as it happens, nor to the circumstances of particular persons. It must establish general, comprehensive regulations for cases and persons. The only question is, which general rule will accommodate most cases and most persons.

Depend upon it, sir, it is dangerous to open so fruitful a source of controversy and altercation, as would be opened by attempting to alter the qualifications of voters. There will be no end of it. New claims will arise. Women will demand a vote. Lads from 12 to 21 will think their rights not enough attended to, and every man, who has not a farthing, will demand an equal voice with any other in all acts of state. It tends to confound and destroy all distinctions, and prostrate all ranks, to one common level.

Kurland, Philip B./ Lerner, Ralph (Hrsg.): ,'The Founders' Constitution. Chicago: University of Chicago Press 1987, S. 394–396.

M5 Land of the Unfree

Four groups – Negroes, servants, women, and minors – together comprised approximately 80 per cent of the two and a half million Americans in the year 1776. The legal doctrine applied to these classes excluded them from the category of persons who should enjoy the "inalienable rights" of which the Declaration speaks. But perhaps the most significant mark of their unfreedom was their usual lack of a right to vote, for the privilege of consenting to the laws was the essential right of a free man in Lockean theory. [...]

A fifth group of colonial Americans, adult white males with little or no property, was deprived of the vote in colonial elections and so fell short of full liberty in the Lockean sense. But they were privileged above the other unfree groups since they were legally entitled to acquire property and were protected from physical abuse except such as was administered by public authority after trial as punishment for offenses against the state. Some of these disenfranchised males were idiots [this is the proper technical term for mentally handicapped persons at the time of this article (1973), Anm. d. Verf.], invalids, or residents of workhouses. Others were simply too poor to qualify under the arbitrary property requirements of the various electoral laws. Statistically they are the least significant of the unfree [...] If they are added to the 80 per cent of the population in the other unfree categories, which were limited not merely in their political rights but in their rights to personal liberty and property as well, then only 10 to 15 per cent of the American population remain to qualify as "freemen" in the fullest sense.

Depauw, L. G. (1987) 'Land of the Unfree: Legal Limitations on Liberty in Pre-Revolutionary America', in L. Dinnerstein and K. T. Jackson (eds) American vistas 1607–1877 (fifth edition, New York and Oxford: Oxford University Press), pp. 89–99 [originally published in Maryland Historical Magazine 68 (1973)], Exzerpt zitiert nach: William Dudley (Hrsg.): The American Revolution. Opposing Viewpoints. San Diego: Greenhaven Press 1992, S. 248.

1.5 The American Revolution – a Historical Analysis

M1 The Wars of the American Revolution

E. Wayne Carp, Professor of History at Pacific Lutheran University, USA

One of the central myths that many Americans entertain about the Revolutionary War is that victory over the British redcoats was quick and easy. In this nationalist version of history, a united, freedom-loving people rose up in righteous anger at the King's tyrannical actions, grabbed their trusty flintlocks, hid behind trees and walls, defeated the dull British soldiers who were sitting ducks in their scarlet uniforms, and established the United States of America. Throughout the story, there is a certain inevitability about American victory.

This story raises many problems. If victory was so easy, why did it take eight and a half years for the Americans to win it? There is also the question of Valley Forge, which Americans have always interpreted as a parable of courage over adversity. But while one can admire Americans' fortitude, there is still the real question: why were Continental Army soldiers lacking clothing and shoes and starving to death in the middle of a prosperous country?

These questions and others have prompted modern historians to revise our understanding of the Revolutionary War. We now recognize that the war affected almost everyone in America. Of the ten wars that Americans have fought, only the Civil War saw more American military deaths per 10,000 citizens. And, except for the Vietnam War, the Revolution was the longest war Americans ever fought.

Historians also began to recognize that the American Revolutionary War was a complex event that belies a simplistic nationalist view. They now argue that the American Revolutionary War contained many *different* wars. It was, first, a war for national independence. Although this type of war is taken for granted by Americans today, it must be remembered that the Revolutionary War was the first in which colonies successfully rebelled against an imperial power. As a result, the American Revolution became an inspiration to other colonial peoples in the nineteenth century. This was especially true for Spanish-American liberators like Simon Bolivar who, in throwing off Spanish rule, looked to the example of the American Revolution.

Second, the American Revolutionary War was a civil war. Rather than a country united against the British, Americans were divided over whether the colonies should leave the British empire. We now know that in every part of the United States, but especially in the South after 1778 (when the British transferred its military operations to that region), Americans fought Americans. Sometimes, American family members fought each other, as fathers sided with the British and sons with the Americans (or visa versa). Historians now believe that forty percent of Americans were patriots; twenty percent were Loyalists, who supported the British; and forty percent were neutral, preferring to be left alone during the hostilities. Almost 18,000 Loyalists actually joined the British army and fought against Americans. These conflicts were often extremely violent and bitter, reminiscent of ethnic conflicts between Serbians and Bosnians today.

Third, the American Revolution was also a world war. With the American victory at Saratoga in 1778, France entered the war on the American side. The French wanted to avenge its defeat in 1763 at the hands of the British in the Seven Years' War. It had been secretly supplying the Americans with military supplies since 1775 awaiting an opportunity to side openly with the revolting Americans. By 1780, both Holland and Spain joined the French and Americans. [...] With their seafaring fleets, America's European allies attacked British possessions in the West Indies, Africa, and India, thus spreading the war over the face of the globe.

Historians also stress the importance of the direct assistance that the European allies gave to the Americans in their victory over the British. It is probably not going too far to say that America owes its independence to foreign intervention and aid, especially from France. The French monarchy sent arms, clothing, and ammunition to America; it also sent soldiers and the French Navy. Most importantly, the French kept the United States government solvent by lending it the money to keep the Revolution alive. The magnitude of French support of the American Revolution can be glimpsed at the battle of Yorktown. There, the majority of George Washington's 15,000 man Continental Army were French soldiers. Washington's men were clothed by the French, the rifles they used were French, and French gold paid their wages. Nor must we forget that it was the French Navy that trapped Cornwallis's soldiers at Yorktown by preventing English ships sent from New York from rescuing the British army. Perhaps the final irony of the French monarchy's assistance to America (and proving once again that no good deed goes unpunished) is that it led to the financial collapse of the French *ancien regime*. And the bankruptcy of Louis XVI was one of the major causes of the French Revolution.

The importance of foreign intervention cannot be overemphasized. Many Americans assume that Yorktown ended the American Revolution. But technically, the British could have continued fighting. Ten thousand soldiers remained in New York City under General Clinton. Thousands more could have been sent from England. But just as America in 1973 made peace in Vietnam, the British in 1783 decided to make peace with America. It would do so for both political and military reasons. Attacked in Parliament and spread thin by attacks in all parts of its empire, the British ministry decided to cut its losses in America and grant independence to its former colony. It did so primarily in order to consolidate its own military forces and fight the French and Spanish. The British went on to defeat both European powers and preserve what would come to be called the Second British Empire.

Finally, the American Revolution was a war of ideas. The new nation which declared itself independent in 1776 was founded upon the "natural rights" philosophy of John Locke, the English political theorist and philosopher. Following ideas and values embedded in the Declaration of Independence, Americans went to war to defend the inalienable rights of man to life, liberty, and the pursuit of happiness and that all men were created equal. Underlying this theory of natural rights was the contract theory of government that postulated that government was a voluntary agreement between a ruler and the people and that when the ruler violated that contract the people had the right of revolution. To launch a revolution, and fight a war for political principles was a new development in the world. Certainly, in the eighteenth century, Europeans fought wars for dynastic ambition or

economic gain. The American Revolution's emphasis on self-rule and the right of revolution was a standing challenge to the existing European order that would not go unnoticed. The world of kings and lords, hierarchy and inequality, would never be the same again.
http://revolution.h-net.msu.edu/essays/carp.html

M2 Modern Views in an American History Book

Howard Spodek (Professor of History and Geography at Temple University / College of Liberal Arts, USA) in his 'World's History', 1998

The American Revolution went further in establishing political democracy than had the Glorious Revolution in England. It abolished the monarchy entirely, replacing it with an elected government. Having declared that "all men are created equal," with unalienable rights not only to life and liberty, but also to the vague but seductive "pursuit of happiness," the revolutionaries now set out to consolidate their commitments in a new legal structure. [...]
After the Authorities won their war for independence, 1775–81, and, in 1783, achieved a peace treaty with Britain, political leaders of the thirteen colonies that had fought met in Philadelphia to establish a framework for their new nation. They drafted a new Constitution in 1789, and a Bill of Rights, which was ratified in 1791. The American Bill of Rights, the first ten amendments to the Constitution, guaranteed to Americans not only the basic rights enjoyed by the British at the time, but more: freedom of religion, [...] press, assembly, and petition; the right to bear arms; protection against unreasonable searches and against cruel and unusual punishment; and the right to a speedy and proper trial by a jury of peers. The states individually set the rules for voting, and many, but not all, removed the property requirements. By 1800 Vermont had instituted universal manhood suffrage, and South Carolina, Pennsylvania, New Hampshire, and Delaware extended the vote to virtually every adult white male taxpayer.
Historians of the early United States situate the more radical American approach to political liberty in at least four factors: cultural, economic, social and philosophical. [...]
The American Revolution, in addition to securing British rights for Americans, was also, and perhaps more importantly, the first modern anti-Colonial revolution. The trade and taxation policies imposed by Britain had pushed businessmen and artisans into opposition to British rule. Other nations, notably France, eager to embarrass Britain and to detach its most promising colonies, provided financial and military support, which helped the Americans to win their independence.
One of the goals of the Revolution was to open the North American continent west of the Appalachian Mountains to settlement. The British prohibition on this westward movement had stood in stark contrast to Spanish and Portuguese settlement policy in Latin America. As the newly independent Americans migrated westward, annexing land as they went, they began to develop imperial interests that were expressed in the mystique of "Manifest Destiny." [...]
Over the centuries America continued to serve as an inspiration to anti-Colonial forces, Jawaharlal Nehru, leading India's twentieth-century struggle for independence from Britain, cited the American Revolution as a model for his own country. [...]
The American Revolution, however, did not bring democracy to everyone. The greatest short-coming was the American perpetuation of slavery. The system was finally ended only by the American Civil War, 1861–1865. [...]
Even afterward, racial discrimination characterized American law until the 1960s and continues to mark American practice up to the present. The status of the Native American population actually worsened after the Revolution, as settlers of European extraction headed west, first by wagon train and later by railroad. They slaughtered American Indians, pushed them out of the way, confined them to remote, semi-barren reservations, destroyed the buffalo herds on which their nomadic existence depended, yet dis-

couraged the preservation of their separate cultures and languages. For the indigenous Indians the effects of the Revolution were exactly opposite to those of the settlers: expansion became contraction, democracy became tyranny, prosperity became poverty, and liberty became confinement. [...]

How did America reconcile its ideals of equality and liberty with the enslavement of blacks and the confinement of Indians at home? It did so by considering non-whites and non-Europeans as "other" – that is, as not quite equal biologically. Race was often used as a definition, usually made by a quick, if approximate and sometimes inaccurate, visual measure, and often as a legal standard. [...] If non-whites were considered not quite equal biologically, the unalienable right to liberty could be abridged. Once the revolutionary principle of equality was accepted in America and elsewhere, the battle was drawn between those who wished to narrow its application to an "in-group" while excluding "others" and those who wished to apply it to all peoples. That battle continues today, in law and in practice, in the United States and around the globe.

Spodek, Howard: The World's History. Combined Edition. New Jersey: Prentice Hall 1998, S. 474–476.

2. The Industrial Revolution

2.1 The Spirit of Progress

The age of industrialization is unique in history. Never before had human beings seen the world change so drastically within so short a period of time. Never before had all aspects of life changed almost simultaneously, sometimes beyond recognition: the world of work, living conditions, even the natural environment. We are talking about the central and western European world of the 19th century – and about the United States. In Great Britain this phase had already started in the second half of the 18th century, in Germany the middle of the 19th century was the 'take-off period' of the industrial revolution.
Industrialization did not just happen: Man no longer waited for the world to develop but actively changed his world. The medieval idea that the world basically was static had been giving way to the idea of progress ever since the scientific revolution and the age of enlightenment provided the philosophical background to this 'can-do mentality'.
Analyzing the Industrial Revolution we find that it is multi-facetted. There are, for example, the

- Agricultural Revolution
- Revolution in Technology and Production
- Demographic Revolution
- Transport Revolution
- Revolution of Ideas.

The age of industrialization brought about the transformation from agricultural societies to industrialized societies, from village-life to city-life. Life expectancy rose and the population figures in all the industrializing countries exploded. In the end it was no longer agriculture that fed people but trade and industry. Imagine that whereas in 1820 the horse had still been the fastest means of transport, one could travel by train at a speed of more than 100 km/h. by the end of the 19th century. What is more: there were already the first cars to be seen and the age-old dream of flying was well within reach. The first plane, the Wright brothers' *Kitty Hawk*, would take off in the United States in 1903.

The Centennial Mirror – originally a poster for the first American World Exhibition in Philadelphia in 1776 – introduces us to the 19th century spirit of progress and to the changes that were affecting all areas of life. The OECD data on the development of worldwide per capita GDP through the ages exemplify the changing role of Europe in the world.

M1 The Centennial Mirror

The Centennial Mirror originally was an oil print, a poster inviting the public to take a look at the wonders to be marvelled at during the first American World exhibition in Philadelphia in 1876.

M2 The Dynamics of World Economies
World Per Capita GDP, 20 Countries and Regional Averages, 1-2001 AD (in standardized dollars). Angus Maddison (*1926), Prof. em. of Economics and long-time head statistician at the OECD in Paris, compiled these figures from all the best information internationally available.

	1	1000	1500	1600	1700	1820	1870	1913	1950	1973	2001
Austria			707	837	993	1.218	1.863	3.465	3.706	11.235	20.225
Belgium			875	976	1.144	1.319	2.692	4.220	5.402	12.170	20.924
Denmark			738	875	1.039	1.274	2.003	3.912	6.943	11.945	23.160
Finland			453	538	638	781	1.140	2.111	4.253	11.085	20.344
France			727	841	910	1.135	1.876	3.485	5.271	13.114	21.092
Germany			688	791	910	1.077	1.839	1.648	3.881	11.966	18.677
Italy			1.100	1.100	1.100	1.117	1.499	2.564	1.502	10.634	19.010
Netherlands			761	1381	2130	1.838	2.757	4.049	5.996	13.082	21.722
Norway			695	821	977	1.198	1.662	3.096	6.739	13.493	20.562
Switzerland			632	750	890	1.090	2.102	4.266	9.064	18.204	22.264
United Kingdom			714	971	1250	1.706	3.190	-1.931	6.939	12.025	20.127
12 Country Average			**798**	**908**	**1.033**	**1.245**	**2.088**	**3.688**	**5.018**	**12.156**	**20.024**
Portugal			606	740	819	923	975	1.250	2.086	7.063	14.229
Spain			601	853	853	1.008	1.207	2.056	2.189	7.661	15.639
Other			472	525	584	711	1.027	1.840	2.538	7.611	15.989
West European average	**450**	**400**	**771**	**890**	**998**	**1.204**	**1.960**	**3.458**	**4.579**	**11.416**	**19.256**
Eastern Europe	**400**	**400**	**496**	**548**	**606**	**683**	**937**	**1.695**	**2.111**	**4988**	**6.027**
Former USSR	**400**	**400**	**499**	**552**	**610**	**688**	**943**	**1.488**	**2.841**	**6059**	**4.626**
United States			400	400	527	1.257	2.445	5.301	9.561	16.689	27.918
Other Western Offshoots			400	400	408	761	2.245	4.752	7.425	13.399	21.718
Average Western Offshoots	**400**	**400**	**400**	**400**	**476**	**1.202**	**2.419**	**5.233**	**9.268**	**16.179**	**26.943**
Mexico			425	454	568	751	674	1.732	2.365	4.815	7.089
Other Latin America			410	431	502	663	683	1.424	2.536	4.426	5.508
Latin American Average	**400**	**400**	**416**	**438**	**527**	**692**	**681**	**1.481**	**2.506**	**4.504**	**5.811**
Japan	400	425	500	520	570	669	737	1.387	1.921	11.434	20.683
China	450	450	600	600	600	600	530	552	539	839	3.583
India	450	450	550	550	550	533	533	673	619	853	1.957
Other Asia	450	450	565	565	565	584	643	882	926	2.019	3.998
Asian average (excl. Japan)	**450**	**450**	**572**	**575**	**571**	**577**	**550**	**658**	**634**	**1.226**	**3.256**
Africa	**430**	**425**	**414**	**422**	**421**	**420**	**500**	**637**	**894**	**1.410**	**1.489**
World	**445**	**336**	**566**	**595**	**615**	**667**	**875**	**1.525**	**2.111**	**4.091**	**6.049**

M3 The Unbound Prometheus

In his standard work 'The Unbound Prometheus' (1969) David Landes (*1924), Harvard University, puts in a nutshell the interrelated facets of the Industrial Revolution

The heart of the Industrial Revolution was an interrelated succession of technological changes. The material advances took place in three areas: (1) there was a substitution of mechanical devices for human skills: (2) inanimate power; in particular steam – took the place of human and animal strength; (3) there was a marked improvement in the getting and working of raw materials, especially in what are now known as the metallurgical and chemical industries.

Concomitant with these changes in equipment and process went new forms of industrial organization. The size of the productive unit grew: machines and power both required and made possible the concentration of manufacture, and shop and home workroom gave way to mill and factory. [...]

Change begat change. For one thing, many technical improvements were feasible only after advances in associated fields. The steam engine is a classic example of this technological interrelatedness: it was impossible to produce an effective condensing engine until better methods of metal working could turn out accurate cylinders. For another, the gains in productivity and output of a given innovation inevitably exerted pressure on related industrial operations. The demand for coal pushed mines deeper until water seepage became a serious hazard; the answer was the creation of a more efficient pump, the atmospheric steam engine. A cheap supply of coal proved a godsend to the iron industry, which was stifling for lack of fuel. In the meantime, the invention and diffusion of machinery in the textile manufacture and other industries created a new demand for energy, hence for coal and steam engines; and these engines, and the machines themselves, had a voracious appetite for iron, which called for further coal and power. Steam also made possible the factory city, which used unheard-of quantities of iron (hence coal) in its many storied mills and its water and sewage systems. At the same time, the processing of the flow of manufactured commodities required great amounts of chemical substances: alkalis, acids, and dyes, most of them consuming mountains of steel in the making. And all of these products-iron, textiles, chemicals-depended on large-scale movements of goods on land and on sea, from the sources of the raw materials into the factories and out again to near and distant markets. The opportunity thus created and the possibilities of the new technology combined to produce the railroad and steamship. Much of course added to the demand for iron and fuel while expanding the market for factor products. And so on, in ever-widening circles.

In this sense, the Industrial Revolution marked a major turning point in man's history. To that point, the advances of commerce and industry, however gratifying and impressive, were essentially superficial: more wealth, more goods, prosperous cities, merchant nabobs. The world had seen other periods of industrial prosperity – in medieval Italy and Flanders, for example – and had seen the line of economic advance recede in each case: in the absence of qualitative changes, of improvements in productivity, there could be no guarantee that mere quantitative gains would be consolidated. It was the Industrial Revolution that initiated a cumulative self-sustaining advance in technology whose repercussions would be felt in all aspects of economic life. [...] The result has been an enormous increase in the output and variety of goods and services, and that alone has changed man's way of life more than anything since the discovery of fire: the Englishman of 1750 was closer in material things to Caesar's legionnaires than to his own great-grandchildren. These material advances in turn have provoked and promoted a large complex of economic, social, political, and cultural changes, which have reciprocally influenced the rate and course of technological development.

David S. Landes (1972; orig. 1969): The Unbound Prometheus: Technological Change and Industrial development in Western Europe from 1750 to the Present, Cambridge University Press, Cambridge, pp.1–5.

2.2 The Agricultural Revolution: A Revolution in Organization, in Farming and Breeding Methods

Without the Agricultural Revolution the Industrial Revolution would perhaps not have taken place. In history the main problem had always been to produce enough food to keep people from starvation; basically there was subsistence farming. Until roughly the late 17th century it took the surplus production of four farming families to feed one non-farming family. Agriculture did not produce enough food to allow much more than 25 % of the population to do jobs in trade and industry. The low intensity agricultural system, the three field crop rotation system meant that at any given time one third of the farmland remained uncultivated (fallow). Obviously there was much room for higher farming productivity.

If the demand for more workers in road construction, textile mills and factories was to be met there had to be a more efficient farming system, so that more food could be produced by a lower percentage of the population. In England, since the 17th century, there had been a trend towards scientifically planned high intensity agriculture. The old three-field crop rotation system was given up in favor of a new four-field crop rotation without fallow. This meant that there was no longer the need for each farmer to own strips of land in each of the three farming sections around the village. So called enclosures (= Flurbereinigung) saw to it that each farmer now had compact tracts of land. The enclosures increased production not only because there was no fallow land anymore. It also increased because the common land where everybody had been allowed to graze their animals and to collect firewood was abolished and in the process of land redistribution turned into farmland or into pasture for sheep.

The smaller farmers who had needed the commons to survive were forced to look for alternative occupations in addition to or instead of farming. But the remaining larger farmers could work their land much more efficiently. Productivity was increased especially with the use of new tools and, later, with newly invented machines and systematic research by early agricultural scientists; e.g. the ploughed acreage per day went up from 0.4 ha in 1700 (using oxen) to 0.8 ha in 1800 (using horses) to 5.0 ha in 1850 (using the steam engine). With the development from the wooden plough via the iron plough to the steam plough, from the sickle to the steam harvester the yield per acre went up and the number of farm workers needed went down.

Those who wanted to be successful in agriculture had to invest a lot of money, i.e. farming became capital intensive. In the process of the Agricultural Revolution, especially in a second phase when (in the 19th century) the secrets of fertilizers were discovered, large numbers of workers from the farming areas became available for the newly established cotton mills, the coal mines and the factories. England took the lead in this development; it also took place in other Western and Central European countries but with a considerable time lag. Nowhere were the consequences of the Agricultural Revolution as drastic as in England: The logic of capitalism, i.e. the new logic of free trade, competition and of the (international) division of labor was so rigorously applied that by the end of the 19th century there were hardly any farmers left – less than 10 % of the workforce. The population could be fed much more cheaply by imports from the colonies. A peasant subsistence economy had changed into a capitalist agricultural system. The wealth of the country which once had almost totally depended on its agricultural production was now a matter of its industrial production, agriculture accounting for only a low percentage of the gross national product.

M1 The Agricultural Revolution

Mark Overton, Professor of Economic and Social History at the University of Exeter, is one of the foremost experts on the agrarian history of England. In the introduction to his book Agricultural Revolution in England (1996) he outlines major aspects of the agrarian revolution and their mutual interdependence.

There is a remarkable consensus, which stretches back to the earliest writing on the subject, that the essence of the 'agricultural revolution' was an increase in cereal yields per acre, that is the amount of grain that could be produced from a given area of land sown with a particular crop. The mechanism for raising yields was described by William Marshall in 1795: 'No dung – no turnips – no bullocks – no barley no clover – nor ... wheat.' He was describing a crop rotation that became known as the Norfolk four-course, which was regarded by contemporary agricultural writers as responsible for unprecedented improvements in crop yields, and farm output. It is not surprising, therefore, that the set of principles underlying the rotation are regarded by historians as the cornerstones of the 'agricultural revolution'. [...]

Turnips and clover are considered important because they enabled English agriculture to break out of the 'closed curcuit' which prevented increases in output other than by extending the cultivated area. [...] When the land is cultivated under a crop rotation where two or three grain crops are followed by a fallow. Fallow is land left uncropped. [...] The fallow was necessary to help the fertility of the soil recover after nutrients had been removed by grain crops. Fertility is also seen as a function of the amount of manure, which in turn depends on the amount of fodder available for animals to eat. Most of this fodder came from meadow and pasture, but a weedy fallow would also have provided some food. The productivity of' this system is equated with grain yields per acre, which are determined by soil fertility. Assuming the cultivated area to be fixed, any increase in the proportion of land under grain would reduce the proportion of fallow or pasture, so reducing fodder, fertility and yields. Thus, the increase in grain output accruing from an increase in the area under grain crops would be offset by a fall in yields per acre as a result of the reduction in fertility.

This vicious circle was broken by replacing fallows with fodder crops. The new crops, turnips and clover, had a fourfold impact. First, they replaced the unproductive fallow with a growing crop. Second, the loss of fodder from the fallow was more than compensated for by the new supplies of fodder which increased manure production and therefore fertility. Third, clover has the valuable property of fixing atmospheric nitrogen into the soil. Nitrogen is a major plant food but cereal crops cannot make use of atmospheric nitrogen and must absorb nitrogen through their roots in the form of nitrogen salts, such as ammonium nitrate. As with other leguminous plants (such as peas and beans) clover converts atmospheric nitrogen into nitrates in the soil; in effect, it makes fertiliser. Thus, the loss of the `rest' given by the fallow was compensated by the fixing of atmospheric nitrogen by clover. Fourth, turnips acted as a `cleaning crop'. The fallow period had presented an opportunity to eradicate perennial weeds through ploughing, but turnips achieved the same effect by smothering weeds, and could be easily hoed when sown in rows. Turnips also provided winter fodder for animals since they could remain in the ground during the first half of the winter. Thus, the way was open for an ascending spiral of progress in so far as more food could be produced from the same area of land. There is much truth in this conventional view, but it is an oversimplification [...].

Three sets of criteria can be identified in the literature as implicitly or explicitly constituting the grounds for claiming an 'agricultural revolution'. The first of these embraces a wide variety of changes in farming techniques. These include the introduction of new fodder crops and new crop rotations, the watering of meadows, the improvement of livestock breeds and the introduction of ma-

chinery. The second is the fact that English agriculture was successful in responding to the challenge of feeding a growing population, an argument that has been employed for both the sixteenth and seventeenth centuries, and for the century after 1750. The third is the view that an 'agricultural revolution' is best characterised as an increase in output brought about by improvements in productivity. [...]
The argument adopted in this book is that the agricultural sector of the economy underwent two related transformations during the period 1500–1850. The first, which was largely a product of the period after 1700, enabled English agriculture to increase output to unprecedented levels, and sustain that output in the face of ever-increasing demand. In 1500 roughly 80 per cent of the population were working in agriculture; by 1850 the proportion was around 20 per cent. This rise in the productivity of labour in agriculture meant that an increasing proportion of the population were working in the industrial and tertiary sectors of the economy; in other words that an industrial revolution was taking place.
[...] By 1850, the majority of farmers produced much more than they needed for themselves, and were businessmen farming for the market. Markets and marketing had been revolutionised; private property rights were universal, and farming was dominated by the tripartite class structure of landlord, tenant farmer and labourer. The period during which these changes occurred was a more protracted one, and unlike the first transformation there are strong grounds for claiming it was underway by the mid-seventeenth century.

Mark Overton: The Agricultural Revolution in England, Cambridge University Press, Cambridge 1996, pp. 1–3; 7–9.

2.3 Britain: The Workshop of the World. The Revolution in Technology and Production

2.3.1 The Textile Industry

Britain, more specifically England, took the lead in industrialization. We can date the take-off phase in the 2nd half of the 18th century. By the mid-nineteenth century Britain had become the 'Workshop of the World', representing more than half of world industrial production.
Looking at the development of the city of Leeds one can see the changes which were brought about first by the rise of the textile industry and then by the emergence of the engineering industries.
The textile industry was the first so-called trigger industry of the Industrial Revolution. A steadily rising population at home and expanding markets in the rapidly developing North American colonies (1700: 275,000; 1776: 2,500,000) led to an ever stronger demand for textiles (the share of exports to North America rose from 5 % of British exports in 1710 to 22 % in 1774) ; enclosures allowed more sheep to be raised and more wool to be produced; newly invented tools and machines turned the production of textiles from a cottage business into a highly mechanized industry. In a second phase (in the 19th century) there was the rise of the cotton-based textile industry, finding its markets world-wide.
New inventions almost necessarily led to further inventions. The spinning jenny, for example, provided the market with so much yarn that hand looms could no longer cope with the quantities delivered. A bottleneck situation in weaving was created; the resulting pressure led to improvements in weaving, e. g. to the power loom.

M1 The Growth of a City

a) Leeds mid – 18th Century, pen drawing

b) The city of Leeds official website tells the story of a city in the Industrial Revolution that experiences the change from pastoral idyll to industrial city.

1700–1780

The woollen cloth market continues to grow, and moves to purpose built Cloth Halls. The business of the town is dominated by the wealthy cloth merchants, who trade both in Britain and abroad. Cloth manufacture is still a cottage industry, and dyeing and finishing are carried out in small workshops attached to the merchants' houses.

1780–1850

The Industrial Revolution comes to Leeds. Matthew Murray pioneers the engineering industry in Leeds, Benjamin Gott brings all the processes of woollen manufacture under one roof at his factory at Bean Ing, and John Marshall sets up as a flax spinner in Holbeck. The population grows as the new industries demand a larger workforce. The engineering, chemical and leather industries all expand, and three new industries, clothing manufacture, footwear manufacture and printing grow in importance.

1850–1900

The textile industry begins to decline, but the engineering, chemical and leather industries all expand, and three new industries, clothing manufacture, footwear manufacture and printing grow in importance. This results in a diverse economy. Leeds becomes 'the city that makes everything.'

http://www.leeds.gov.uk/discover/discovery.asp?page=2003219_348858059

c) Population of Leeds

1685:	2,000
1801:	94,421
1831:	183,015
1881:	433,607

d) Late 19th century pen drawing Leeds

M2 Leeds Woollen Workers Petition, 1786

This petition by workers in Leeds (a major center of wool manufacture in Yorkshire) appeared in a local newspapers in 1786. They are complaining about the effects of machines on the previously well-paid skilled workers.

To the Merchants, Clothiers and all such as wish well to the Staple Manufactory of this Nation.

The Scribbling-Machines have thrown thousands of your petitioners out of employ, whereby they are brought into great distress, and are not able to procure a maintenance for their families, and deprived them of the opportunity of bringing up their children to labour: [...]

The number of Scribbling-Machines extending about seventeen miles south-west of LEEDS, exceed all belief, being no less than *one hundred and seventy*! and as each machine will do as much work in twelve hours, as ten men can in that time do by hand, (speaking within bounds) and they working night and day, one machine will do as much work in one day as would otherwise employ twenty men. [...]

We wish to propose a few queries to those who would plead for the further continuance of these machines:

Men of common sense must know, that so many machines in use, take the work from the hands employed in Scribbling, – and who did that business before machines were invented.

How are those men, thus thrown out of employ to provide for their families; – and what are they to put their children apprentice to, that the rising generation may have something to keep them at work, in order that they may not be like vagabonds strolling about in idleness? Some say, Begin and learn some other business. – Suppose we do; who will maintain our families, whilst we undertake the arduous task; and when we have learned it, how do we know we shall be any better for all our pains; for by the time we have served our second apprenticeship, another machine may arise, which may take away that business also; so that our families, being half pined whilst we are learning how to provide them with bread, will be wholly so during the period of our third apprenticeship.

But what are our children to do; are they to be brought up in idleness? Indeed as things are, it is no wonder to hear of so many executions; for our parts, though we may be thought illiterate men, our conceptions are, that bringing children up to industry, and keeping them employed, is the way to keep them from falling into those crimes, which an idle habit naturally leads to.

These things impartially considered will we hope, be strong advocates in our favour; and we conceive that men of sense, religion and humanity, will be satisfied of the reasonableness, as well as necessity of this address, and that their own feelings will urge them to espouse the cause of us and our families –

Signed, in behalf of THOUSANDS, by Joseph Hepworth Thomas Lobley Robert Wood Thos. Blackburn

From J. F. C. Harrison, Society and Politics in England, 1780–1960 (New York: Harper & Row, 1965), pp. 71–72. Taken from: Modern History Sourcebook: http://www.fordham.edu/halsall/mod/1786machines.html

M3 Letter from Leeds Cloth Merchants, 1791

This statement by the Cloth Merchants of Leeds (a major center of wool manufacture in Yorkshire) defended the use of machines.

At a time when the People, engaged in every other Manufacture in the Kingdom, are exerting themselves to bring their Work to Market at reduced Prices, which can alone be effected by the Aid of Machinery, it certainly is not necessary that the Cloth Merchants of Leeds, who depend chiefly on a Foreign Demand, where they have for Competitors the Manufacturers of other Nations, whose Taxes are few, and whose manual Labour is only Half the Price it bears here, should have Occasion to defend a Conduct, which has for its Aim the Advantage of the Kingdom in general, and of the Cloth Trade in particular; yet anxious to prevent Misrepresentations, which have usually attended the Introduction of the most useful Machines, they wish to remind the Inhabitants of this Town, of the Advantages derived to every flourishing Manufacture from the Application of Machinery; they instance that of Cotton in particular, which in its internal and foreign Demand is nearly alike to our own, and has in a few Years by the Means of Machinery advanced to its present Importance, and is still increasing.

If then by the Use of Machines, the Manufacture of Cotton, an Article which we import, and are supplied with from other Countries, and which can every where be procured on equal Terms, has met with such amazing Success, may not greater Advantages be reasonably expected from cultivating to the utmost the Manufacture of Wool, the Produce of our own Island, an Article in Demand in all Countries, almost the universal Clothing of Mankind?

In the Manufacture of Woollens, the Scribbling Mill, the Spinning Frame, and the Fly Shuttle, have reduced manual Labour nearly One third, and each of them at its-first Introduction carried an Alarm to the Work People, yet each has contributed to advance the Wages and to increase the Trade, so that if an Attempt was now made to deprive us of the Use of them, there is no Doubt, but every Person engaged in the Business, would exert himself to defend them.

From these Premises, we the undersigned Merchants, think it a Duty we owe to ourselves, to the Town of Leeds, and to the Nation at large, to declare that we will protect and support the free Use of the proposed Improvements in Cloth-Dressing, by every legal Means in our Power; and if after all, contrary to our Expectations, the Introduction of Machinery should for a Time occasion a Scarcity of Work in the Cloth Dressing Trade, we have unanimously agreed to give a Preference to such Workmen as are now settled Inhabitants of this Parish, and who give no Opposition to the present Scheme.

Appleby & Sawyer, Bernard Bischoff & Sons, [and 59 other names]

From J. F. C. Harrison, Society and Politics in England, 1780–1960 (New York: Harper & Row, 1965), pp. 72–74. Taken from: Modern History Sourcebook: http://www.fordham.edu/halsall/mod/1791machines.html

M4 Comparative Data on Wool and Cotton in 19th century Europe

a) raw wool output (000 metric tons)	1801	1850	1880	1900	1910
Great Britain	45	60	66	62	52
France	38	28.2	138.2	40.1	34.4
Germany	n.a.	66.6	30.1	154.7	175.7
Italy	n.a.	n.a.	9.6	10.8	14.6

Cipolla, Carlo M.: The Fontana Economic History of Europe, Bd. 2, 1976[3], S. 783.

b) raw cotton consumption (000 metric tons)	1800	1830	1860	1880	1910
Great Britain	13.9	105.6	369.4	605.0	868.8
France	n.a.	33.5	74.1	99.5	231.1
Germany	n.a.	3.9	42.0	134.3	435.4
Italy	n.a.	n.a.	1.8	30.7	186.0
Russia	n.a.	1.8	34.3	109.6	352.2

Cipolla, The Fontana Economic History of Europe, Bd. 2, 1976^3, S. 780

M5 The Physical Deterioration of the Textile Workers

The physical deterioration of the manufacturing class in England was still noticeable in the 1930s, more than a century after the height of the Industrial Revolution. A medical observer's description of what the work did to the worker follows.

Any man who has stood at twelve o'clock at the single narrow door-way, which serves as the place of exit for the hands employed in the great cotton-mills, must acknowledge, that an uglier set of men and women, of boys and girls, taking them in the mass, it would be impossible to congregate in a smaller compass. Their complexion is sallow and pallid--with a peculiar flatness of feature, caused by the want of a proper quantity of adipose substance to cushion out the cheeks. Their stature low--the average height of four hundred men, measured at different times, and different places, being five feet six inches. Their limbs slender, and playing badly and ungracefully. A very general bowing of the legs. Great numbers of girls and women walking lamely or awkwardly, with raised chests and spinal flexures. Nearly all have flat feet, accompanied with a down-tread, differing very widely from the elasticity of action in the foot and ankle, attendant upon perfect formation. Hair thin and straight--many of the men having but little beard, and that in patches of a few hairs, much resembling its growth among the red men of America. A spiritless and dejected air, a sprawling and wide action of the legs, and an appearance, taken as a whole, giving the world but "little assurance of a man," or if so, "most sadly cheated of his fair proportions ..."

Factory labour is a species of work, in some respects singularly unfitted for children. Cooped up in a heated atmosphere, debarred the necessary exercise, remaining in one position for a series of hours, one set or system of muscles alone called into activity, it cannot be wondered at--that its effects are injurious to the physical growth of a child. Where the bony system is still imperfect, the vertical position it is compelled to retain, influences its direction; the spinal column bends beneath the weight of the head, bulges out laterally, or is dragged forward by the weight of the parts composing the chest, the pelvis yields beneath the opposing pressure downwards, and the resistance given by the thigh-bones; its capacity is lessened, sometimes more and sometimes less; the legs curve, and the whole body loses height, in consequence of this general yielding and bending of its parts.

P. Gaskell, The Manufacturing Population of England. London, 1833, pp.161–162, 202–203.
Taken from: http://www.victorianweb.org/victorian/history/workers2.html.

M6 A Cotton Manufacturer on Hours of Labour

John Fielden, although himself a Lancashire factory owner, was one of the staunchest fighters for protective legislation for the cotton worker.

Here, then, is the "curse" of our factory-system; as improvements in machinery have gone on, the "avarice of masters" has prompted many to exact more labour from their hands than they were fitted by nature to perform, and those who have wished for the hours of labour to be less for all ages than the legislature would even yet sanction, have had no alternative but to conform more or less to the prevailing practice, or abandon the trade altogether. This has been the case with regard to myself and my partners. We have never worked more than seventy-one hours a week before Sir JOHN HOBHOUSE'S Act was passed. We then came down to **sixty-nine**; and since Lord ALTHORP's Act was passed, in 1833, we have reduced the time of adults to **sixty-seven and a half hours** a week, and that of children under thirteen years of age to **forty-eight** hours in the week, though to do this latter has, I must admit, subjected us to much inconvenience, but the elder hands to more, inasmuch as the relief given to the child is in some measure imposed on the adult. But the overworking does not apply to children only; the adults are also overworked. The increased speed given to machinery within the last thirty years, has, in very many instances, doubled the labour of both.

John Fielden, M.P., The Curse of the Factory System. London, 1836, pp. 34–35.

M7 Machine-Breakers

The Cotton Times is a website devoted to the history of the Industrial Revolution, especially to the role of the cotton industry.

LANCASHIRE textile workers were notorious for their mistrust of progress and for their violent reaction to anything which they considered threatened their livelihoods. [...]

The biggest revolt against machinery had its beginnings in Nottingham rather than in the textile towns of Lancashire.

It was early in 1811 that Nottingham stocking manufacturers began to receive letters signed by "General Ned Ludd and his Army of Redressers." Ludd probably did not exist, although there is some suggestion that the name was derived from that of a Leicestershire farm labourer who had destroyed some stocking frames about 1782. The legend that grew up about him was that he was a Nottingham youth who had his headquarters in Sherwood Forest, like a latter-day Robin Hood.

Real or not, Ludd had a startling effect on industry in the Midlands. Soon, workers who had seen their wages reduced and their jobs threatened by unskilled rivals began breaking into factories and destroying machines.

Their main targets were the new, wide frames operated by unapprenticed workers, which produced poor quality but cheap stockings. In just three weeks, more than 200 of these frames were destroyed and 400 special constables had to be sworn in to protect the factories.

The Prince Regent offered a £50 reward for information about the Luddites and in February, 1812, as the problem spread North, Spencer Perceval's Government passed the Frame-Breaking Act, which carried the death penalty, and ordered 12,000 troops into the affected areas.

LUDDITES used a sledgehammer and a crowbar to smash power looms in a weaving shed.

But as wheat prices climbed and workers found it virtually impossible to feed their families, neither move had much effect. There were food riots in towns through the North West, and on March 20th, the cotton industry had its first taste of Luddism when William Radcliffe's Stockport power-loom sheds were attacked.

In April, two workers were killed in an attack on a Huddersfield mill, and a week later a mill owner was murdered in the same area. On April 8th, there was a riot at Manchester's Exchange as workers showed what they thought of a plan to send a loyal address to the Prince Regent. [...]

Altogether during that violent summer of 1812, eight Lancashire men were executed and 13 more transported to Australia. But authority quickly tightened its grip.
By early June, 30,000 troops from the Wiltshire, Buckinghamshire, Louth and Stirling regiments were camped on Kersal Moor above Manchester, ready for action, and before winter, Luddism had all but died out.
There were a few more sporadic attacks up to 1816, but to all intents and purposes, General Ludd had retired.

http://www.cottontimes.co.uk/luddo.htm

2.3.2 Coal, Iron and Steel

The second phase of the Industrial Revolution revolved around the coal and iron industries. The new agricultural tools and machines as well as the newly invented machines in the textile industry created an ever-increasing demand for iron which in turn led to the necessity of finding improved methods for producing iron. Coal pits were established and driven deeper into the ground, making it necessary to drain the pits of the ground water – by means of pumps that had to be invented. Soon animal power proved to be no longer sufficient for this job. A new source of power was needed: the steam engine. With these inventions the Industrial Revolution had arrived at a point in its development when a sustained process of innovation and improvement had been set in motion. From then on innovation led to innovation at an ever-increasing speed: The steam engine helped to produce more coal to produce more iron; the steam engine on rails revolutionized transport which in turn led to an enormously increased demand for iron …

M1 Women Miners in the English Coal Pits

Lord Ashley's Mines Commission of 1842 reported to the British Parliament on the conditions in English coal mines. This report lead to a ban on the employment of females and boys under thirteen years of age.

West Riding of Yorkshire: Southern Part – In many of the collieries in this district, as far as relates to the underground employment, there is no distinction of sex, but the labour is distributed indifferently among both sexes, except that it is comparatively rare for the women to hew or get the coals, although there are numerous instances in which they regularly perform even this work. In great numbers of the coalpits in this district the men work in a state of perfect nakedness, and are in this state assisted in their labour by females of all ages, from girls of six years old to women of twenty-one, these females being themselves quite naked down to the waist.
"Girls," says the Sub-Commissioner [J. C. Symons], – regularly perform all the various offices of trapping, hurrying [Yorkshire terms for drawing the loaded coal corves], filling, riddling, tipping, and occasionally getting, just as they are performed by boys. One of the most disgusting sights I have ever seen was that of young females, dressed like boys in trousers, crawling on all fours, with belts round their waists and chains passing between their legs, at day pits at Hunshelf Bank, and in many small pits near Holmfirth and New Mills: it exists also in several other places. I visited the Hunshelf Colliery on the 18th of January: it is a day pit; that is, there is no shaft or descent; the gate or entrance is at the side of a bank, and nearly horizontal. The gate was not more than a yard high, and in some places not above 2 feet. [...]
"In two other pits in the Huddersfield Union I have seen the same sight. In one near New Mills, the chain, passing high up between the legs of two of these girls, had worn large holes in their trousers; and any sight more disgustingly indecent or revolting can scarcely be imagined than these girls at work-no brothel can beat it.

"On descending Messrs Hopwood's pit at Barnsley, I found assembled round a fire a group of men, boys, and girls, some of whom were of the age of puberty; the girls as well as the boys stark naked down to the waist, their hair bound up with a tight cap, and trousers supported by their hips. (At Silkstone and at Flockton they work in their shifts and trousers.) Their sex was recognizable only by their breasts, and some little difficulty occasionally arose in pointing out to me which were girls and which were boys, and which caused a good deal of laughing and joking. In the Flockton and Thornhill pits the system is even more indecent: for though the girls are clothed, at least three-fourths of the men for whom they "hurry" work stark *naked*, or with a flannel waistcoat only, and in this state they assist one another to fill the corves 18 or 20 times a day: I have seen this done myself frequently.

"When it is remembered that these girls hurry chiefly for men who are not their parents; that they go from 15 to 20 times a day into a dark chamber (the bank face), which is often 50 yards apart from any one, to a man working naked, or next to naked, it is not to be supposed but that where opportunity thus prevails sexual vices are of common occurrence. Add to this the free intercourse, and the rendezvous at the shaft or bullstake, where the corves are brought, and consider the language to which the young ear is habituated, the absence of religious instruction, and the early age at which contamination begins, and you will have before you, in the coal-pits where females are employed, the picture of a nursery for juvenile vice which you will go far and we above ground to equal."

Parliamentary Papers, 1842, VoL XVI, pp. 24, 196.

M2 Production Figures: Coal, Iron, and Steel

a) coal output (million metric tons)	1800	1830	1860	1880	1910
Great Britain	11.2	22.8	86.3	158.9	275.4
France	n.a.	2.0	10.0	20.2	39.9
Germany	n.a.	1.9	20.8	65.7	247.5
Italy	n.a.	n.a.	0.04	0.2	0.6
Russia	n.a.	n.a	0.4	3.7	30.2

Cipolla, Carlo M.: The Fontana Economic History of Europe, Bd. 2, 1976[3], S. 770.

b) steel (metric tons)	1870	1880	1890	1900	1910
Great Britain	0.49	1.82	3.19	5.04	6.93
France	–	0.46	0.77	1.70	4.09
Germany	–	0.99	2.89	7.71	16.24
Italy	–	0.15	0.22	0.32	0.98
Russia	–	0.25	0.54	2.35	4.20

Cipolla, The Fontana Economic History of Europe, Bd. 2, 1976[3], S. 775

2.3.3 Demographics

Part of the the Industrial Revolution was the population explosion. In England starting about 1740, in western Europe in the late 18th century, population figures rose steeply – most drastically in the cities, with numbers trebling and quadrupling. Part of the change from an agrarian to an industrialized society was a rapid process of urbanization.
There are a number of reasons responsible for the population explosion:

- The agricultural revolution with its new tools, techniques, crops and an overall increase in led productivity led to more and better food. In England, for example meat consumption per capita rose by 35 % by 1820. Meat became a regular item on the menu.
- The scientific approach to farming meant that man was no longer a helpless victim of the weather and so the constant threat of famine became less pressing because there was less fluctuation from one harvest to the next. People that no longer go hungry can work harder, are healthier and have more resistance to disease.
- In medicine, too, great steps forward were taken: e.g. in 1796 Edward Jenner found a vaccine against smallpox, one of the most deadly diseases of that day. Together, these developments contributed to a significant lowering of the mortality rate especially among children.

However, the process of urbanization cannot just be seen as part of an uninterrupted success story. There were serious problems that urbanization brought with it. In the overcrowded cities people lived densely packed together: there were up to 2000 people per square mile whereas in rural areas there were hardly more than 50 people per square mile. Consequently the cities experienced serious hygiene problems until fresh water supply and sewage systems were introduced after the mid-19th century.
The population explosion becomes even more marked when one considers that in the 19th century many millions of Europeans emigrated to America, which means that the official population figures show only part of the population increase.

M1 Population of European Countries (000 at mid-year)

	1500	1700	1820	1850	1910
United Kingdom	3,942	8,565	21,239	27,181	44,916
France	15,000	21,471	31,250	36,350	41,224
Germany	12,000	15,000	24,905	33,746	62,884
Netherlands	950	1,900	2,333	3,098	5,922
Italy	10,500	13,300	20,176	24,460	36,572

Maddison, The World Economy, OECD 2006, S. 412–421

M2 Average Age of Death

Place	Prefessional/Gentry	Trades men	Labourers
Leeds	44	27	19
Liverpool	35	22	15
Manchester	38	20	17
Wiltshire	50	48	33

Edwin Chadwick, The Sanitary Conditions of the Labouring Population (1842)
Taken from: www.spartacus.schoolnet.co.uk/ITLiverpool.htm

2.4 The Transport Revolution

The rise of the cities and the rise of trigger industries like the textile industry and, later, the coal and iron industry made it necessary to transport raw materials to the mills and factories and made it equally necessary to transport the manufactured products to the consumer. Modern industrial cities no longer had a farming population, so grain and livestock had to be "imported" from the rural areas. It became absolutely essential to find means of cheap and rapid transport for bulky goods - and for travelers as well.
Up to the eve of the Industrial Revolution there had just been local roads full of potholes, unfit for the transport of bulky goods. Now, in a first phase, businessmen asked Parliament for permission to build new and better roads. All through the first half of the 18th century there was a roadbuilding boom turning local markets into regional markets, reducing the time needed to travel from one place to another and leading to a much improved postal service, i.e. a better communication infrastructure.
Transportation costs dropped even more decisively when in the second half of the 18th century canal-building began to boom. Canals allowed for an easier transport of coal and iron from mines to factories. Heavier goods could easily be moved but still the problem remained speed. With the invention of the steam engine it became possible to solve the problem by means of a new system of transportation: the railway.
Many people praised the steam on wheels, others found it difficult to get used to but all in all locomotion revolutionized the 19th century economy and the life of the people. From then on people enjoyed a degree of mobility they could not even have imagined 50 years earlier. The transport revolution of the 19th century, including the introduction of the steamship, led not only to a national division of labor but brought about the emergence of international markets. So by the end of the 19th century it proved no longer necessary for Britain to produce all its own foodstuff, much of it was imported; the agricultural sector became very small in comparison to other European economies.

M1 Turnpikes and Canals

Phyllis Deane was an economist at Newnham College, Cambridge University

a) Private Enterprise: the Dynamo of the Transport Revolution

The interesting thing about the British experience is that it was almost entirely native private enterprise that found both the initiative and the capital to lay down the system of communications which was essential to the British industrial revolution. By the eighteenth century English roads were reputed to be the among the worst in Europe. The growing number of Turnpike Acts gave private enterprise the task of repairing the roads, in turn for the right to collect tolls from users. [...]
Most of the new roads and the best-kept roads led to London, although the influence of other towns – Liverpool, Birmingham and Manchester for example – began to show itself in the quality of their feeder roads as the century wore on. The growing towns called for rapid and regular transport of foodstuff and fuel over distances of 30 to 50 miles or so, and for comfortable, safe and speedy transport of passengers and mail between the main towns; and it was the kind of localized or light traffic that benefited most directly and impressively. [...] If Britain had had to depend on her roads to carry her heavy goods traffic the effective impact of the industrial revolution might well have been delayed until the railway age. [...]
It is to the transformation of the inland system of water navigation that we must look for the most spectacular and typical innovations of this period. The industrial revolution called for a reliable, high-capacity, low-cost-

transport system and this is what the canals provided. Moreover they were of the essence of the industrial revolution in that they were man-made, that they represented an application of scientific knowledge to practical engineering problems, that they catered for a mass market and that they involved heavy capital outlays involving a long-time horizon. The canal age took place mainly in two hectic bursts of construction; the first in the 1760's and early 1770's was inspired by the success of the Duke of Bridgewater's Canal between Worsley coal mine and Manchester; the second started up in the 1780's and became a national mania in the 1790's. It had been preceded by a century and a half of steady river improvement also financed capitalistically by groups of local landowners and businessmen.

The main motive power behind the early development of the canals was the same as that which was gradually pushing up the standards of the roads at this period. It was the growth of the towns. Later the prospectus and needs of large-scale industry helped to rocket the canal age into its grand mania; but, to begin with, the operative force was the towns with their insatiable demand for coal, to supply fuel for domestic needs and for the host of little industries [...] This was one of the crucial bottlenecks that had to be broken before the industrial revolution could take shape in England. It was crucial, first because it removed the main barrier to the urbanisation which is generally associated with industrialization as both cause and effect; and secondly because the first industrial revolution grew up on a basis of coal and iron and it was necessary to be able to move the bulky raw materials and their finished products quickly and cheaply across the face of the country. [...] The coal got to the consumers at reasonable prices, the iron-foundries and potteries could reduce costs, the factory worker could warm his family in winter and still have some money left over to buy the products of British industry and the bread-and-cheese-eating labourers of Southern England could have cooked meals occasionally. In these terms the Canal Age made a massive contribution to the first industrial revolution and was a worthy forerunner of the railway age. [...]

The transport revolution was an absolutely crucial factor in facilitating the cost-reducing innovations which characterized the other transforming sectors of the first industrial revolution.

Phyllis Deane: The First Industrial Revolution, Cambridge University Press, Cambridge 1965, p. 70ff.

b) Weight that could be pulled by Horse, 1807

Speed	By canal	Level RR	Level turnpike, paved
3 mph	39,000 lb	14,000 lb	1,800 lb
4	22,000	"	"
5	13,900	"	"
10	3,500	"	"

Notes: Resistance of canal increases with square of speed. On a well-paved road, the above data apply (4th column). On a dirt road, in which the wagon sinks one inch, the weight is cut in half.

M2 The Development of Transport

Historians have argued that 'a transport revolution' preceded and accompanied all industrial revolutions; economists, similarly, have shown that modern economic growth is correlated positively with transport facilities, and that investment in transport is of strategic and quantitative importance in inducing and sustaining growth. Improved transport is part of the essential infrastructure of an advanced economy, and absorbs today from five to ten per cent of national income. The development of transport, and especially of railways, has been reckoned, by many historians to have been the leading sector in the growth of national economies in the nineteenth century.[...] Improved transport not only directly lowered costs, it also made markets accessible and labour mobile. On occasions changing transport costs led to radical change; for example, when cheaply transported and cheaply produced American wheat reached European markets in the eighteen-eighties leading either to the decline of wheat farming or to its protection.

Social effects were equally impressive: before the industrial revolution, residence and workplace tended to be identical for most people; after the development of the railway, for example, towns grew in size, suburbs separated people's homes not only from places of work but also from other social classes; the railway thus led to the social fragmentation of cities with their spectrum of housing from working-class ghettos, separated by commercial and industrial areas. Some statistics of the growth of transport facilities are impressive enough to underline their importance: European mileage of railways increased from 1,679 in 1840 to 31,885 in 1860 to 135,000 by 1890, and millions of passengers carried over the same period increased from c. 340 to c. 1,750; by 1890, there were in Europe 13,000 miles of canals and over 63,000 miles of navigable rivers; world tonnage of steam shipping increased from c. 30,000 to c. 7.5 millions by 1890, while the tonnage of sea-borne merchandise increased from c. 10 to c. 150 million tons over the same period. Equally important as transport services to shift goods and people was the development of other types of communication, especially those like posts and telegraphs, which reduced the costs of information to producers and consumers. Here, again, there was a decisive break with the past, with the more systematic collection of information and the more effective diffusion of it. The examples of the businessman sending forth cargoes of merchandise to distant and foreign countries, with the flimsiest of information about the market he was serving, and the politician preparing his annual budget, on the basis of economic doctrine rather than of carefully collected statistical information, indicate the revolution of information which was to make these two activities more rational. It was this 'inherent essentiality' of transport and communications which made them from the beginnings of expansion a matter of public interest, and, quickly, of public control. Transport and communication facilities became the first important public enterprises in many industrialising economies, and in others, the first industries to be controlled by extensive government regulation. Transport and communications industries were spearheads of technological advance, large absorbers of capital, and large creators of income.

R.M. Hartwell: The Service Revolution, in: Cipolla, Carlo (ed.), The Fontana Economic History of Europe, vol. 3: The Industrial Revolution, 1976 (1973) (pp. 359–396), pp. 375–377.

M3 Britain's Railway Network

a) Train Passengers in Britain

year	passengers
1838	5 ½ million rail passengers
1845	30 million rail passengers
1855	111 million rail passengers

Atlas of Industrializing Britain, 1780–1914, John Langton/ R.J. Morris (eds.), p. 90.

b) Railway Networks in Europe

railways (in km)	1840	1860	1880	1900	1910
Great Britain	2,390	14,603	25,060	30,079	32,182
France	497	9,167	23,089	38,109	40,484
Germany	469	11,089	33,838	51,678	61,209
Russia	0	1,626	22,865	53,234	66,581

Cipolla, The Fontana Economic History of Europe, Bd. 2, 19763, S. 789.

M4 The Transport Revolution in Perspective

Cromolithograph by Henry Aiken, in Asa Briggs, Iron Bridge to Crystal Palace: Impact and Images of the Industrial Revolution, Thames and Hudson, London 1979, illustration

M5 Travel Times (Hours) from London, 1820–1910

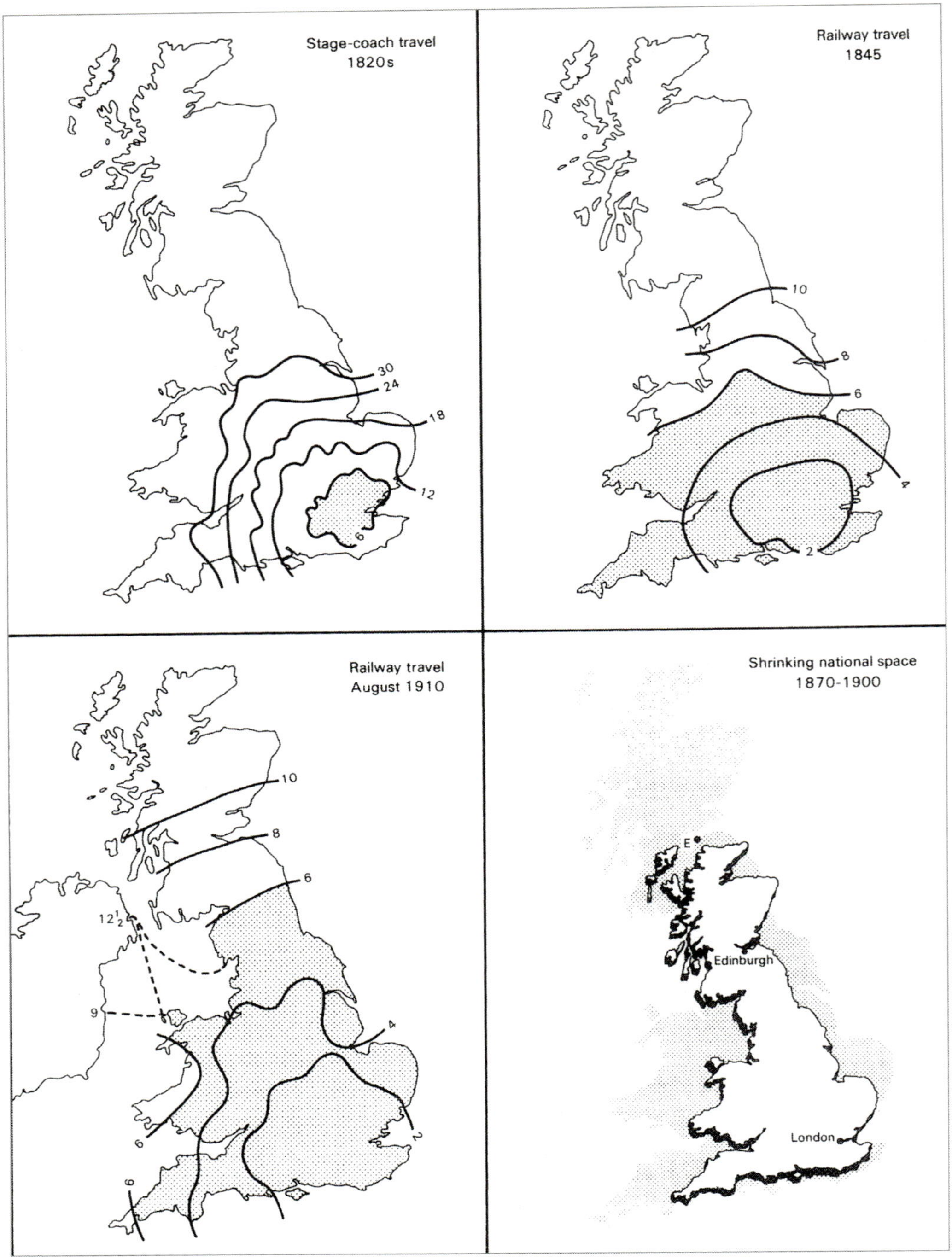

Atlas of Industrializing Britain, 1780–1914, John Langton / R.J. Morris (eds.), Routledge, London 2004, p. 90 [(c 1986) The Economic History Society, and the Historical Geography Research Group of the Institute of British Geographers].

M6 A Literary Train Ride

Trains, train rides and train stations became topics in 'modern' nineteenth century English fiction. Here we have one example by Charles Dickens, one of the foremost English authors.

Mr Dombey Goes Upon a Journey

The power that forced itself upon its iron way – its own – defiant of all paths and roads, piercing through the heart of every obstacle, and dragging living creatures of all classes, ages, and degrees behind it, was a type of the triumphant monster, Death.

Away, with a shriek, and a roar, and a rattle, from the town, burrowing among the dwellings of men and making the streets hum, flashing out into the meadows for a moment, mining in through the damp earth, booming on in darkness and heavy air, bursting out again into the sunny day so bright and wide; away, with a shriek, and a roar, and a rattle, through the fields, through the woods, through the corn, through the hay, through the chalk, through the mould, through the clay, through the rock, among objects close at hand and almost in the grasp, ever flying from the traveller, and a deceitful distance ever moving slowly within him: like as in the track of the remorseless monster, Death!

Through the hollow, on the height, by the heath, by the orchard, by the park, by the garden, over the canal, across the river, where the sheep are feeding, where the mill is going, where the barge is floating, where the dead are lying, where the factory is smoking, where the stream is running, where the village clusters, where the great cathedral rises, where the bleak moor lies, and the wild breeze smooths or ruffles it at its inconstant will; away, with a shriek, and a roar, and a rattle, and no trace to leave behind but dust and vapour: like as in the track of the remorseless monster, Death!

Breasting the wind and light, the shower and sunshine, away, and still away, it rolls and roars, fierce and rapid, smooth and certain, and great works and massive bridges crossing up above, fall like a beam of shadow an inch broad, upon the eye, and then are lost. Away, and still away, onward and onward ever: glimpses of cottage-homes, of houses, mansions, rich estates, of husbandry and handicraft, of people, of old roads and paths that look deserted, small, and insignificant as they are left behind: and so they do, and what else is there but such glimpses, in the track of the indomitable monster, Death!

Away, with a shriek, and a roar, and a rattle, plunging down into the earth again, and working on in such a storm of energy and perseverance, that amidst the darkness and whirlwind the motion seems reversed, and to tend furiously backward, until a ray of light upon the Wet wall shows its surface flying past like a fierce stream, Away once more into the day, and through the day, with a shrill yell of exultation, roaring, rattling, tearing on, spurning everything with its dark breath, sometimes pausing for a minute where a crowd of faces are, that in a minute more are not; sometimes lapping water greedily, and before the spout at which it drinks' has ceased to drip upon the ground, shrieking, roaring, rattling through the purple distance!

Charles Dickens (1812–1870): Dombey and Son, 1846, ch. 20.

2.5 The Business Spirit and Social Responsibility

The economic revolution in terms of industrial production methods and production figures did not only go hand in hand with a revolution in agriculture and with a revolution in living patterns by bringing about large-scale urbanization. These revolutions were both caused by and led to a new frame of mind, a new way of looking at the world. The general spirit of progress has been mentioned earlier on. One must add what Max Weber called 'the spirit of capitalism', i.e. the conscious attempt to structure the world according to the newly identified economic principles as analyzed and described by economists like Adam Smith. But one should also take into account counter-movements. In the history of ideas the bold spirit of progress and of the can-do mentality of materialism was soon matched by the emergence of romanticism that developed a critical perspective on modernization.

M1 Adam Smith, The Wealth of Nations, 1776

Adam Smith (1723–1790), Scottish Enlightenment economist. One of the founders of classical liberal economics, i.e. of laissez faire capitalism.

The Division of Labour

Man has almost constant occasion for the help of his brethren, and it is in vain for him to expect it from their benevolence only. He will be more likely to prevail if he can interest their self-love in his favour, and show them that it is for their own advantage to do for him what he requires of them. Whoever offers to another a bargain of any kind, proposes to do this. Give me what I want, and you shall have this which you want, is the meaning of every such offer; and it is the manner that we obtain from one another the far greater part of those good offices which we stand in need of. It is not from the benevolence of the butcher, the brewer, or the baker that we expect our dinner, but from their regard to their own interest. We address ourselves, not to their humanity but to their self-love. [...]

The Invisible Hand

Every individual is continually exerting himself to find out the most advantageous employment for whatever capital he can command. It is his own advantage, indeed, and not that of the society, which he has in view. But the study of his own advantage naturally, or rather neces-sarily, leads him to prefer that employment which is most advantageous to the society. [...].

As every individual, therefore, endeavours as much as he can both to employ his capital in the support of domestic industry, and so to direct that industry that its produce may be of the greatest value; every individual necessarily labours to render the annual revenue of the society as great as he can. [...] He intends only his own gain, and he is in this, as in many other cases, led by an invisible hand to promote an end which was no part of his intention. Nor is it always the worse for the society that it was no part of it. By pursuing his own interest he frequently promotes that of the society more effectually than when he really intends to promote it. I have never known much good done by those who affected to trade for the public good. ----(book I, 2.2; book IV, 2.4+2.9)

ON PINMAKING

THE greatest improvement in the productive powers of labor, and the greater part of the skill, dexterity, and judgment with which it is anywhere directed, or applied, seem to have been the effects of the division of labour. [...] To take an example, therefore, [...] the trade of the pin-maker; a workman not educated to this business, nor acquainted with the use of the machinery employed in it, could scarce, perhaps, with his utmost industry, make one pin in a day, and certainly could not make twenty. But in the way in which this business is now carried on, not only the whole work is a peculiar trade, but it is divided into a number of branches, of which the greater part are likewise peculiar trades. One man draws out the wire, another straights it, a third cuts it, a fourth points it, a fifth grinds it at the top for receiving, the head; to make the head requires two or three distinct operations; to put it on is a peculiar business, to whiten the pins is another; it is even a trade by itself to put them into the paper; and the important business of making a pin is, in this manner, divided into about eighteen distinct operations, which, in some factories, are all performed by distinct hands, though in others the same man will sometimes perform two or three of them.

I have seen a small manufactory of this kind where ten men only were employed, and where some of them consequently performed two or three distinct operations. But though they were very poor, and therefore but indifferently accommodated with the necessary machinery, they could, when they exerted themselves, make among them about twelve pounds of pins in a day. There are in a pound upwards of four thousand pins of a middling size. Those ten persons, therefore, could make among them upwards of forty-eight thousand pins in a day. Each person, therefore, making a tenth part of forty-eight thousand pins, might be considered as making four thousand eight hundred pins in a day. But if they had all wrought separately and independently, and without any of them having been educated to this peculiar business, they certainly could not each of them have made twenty, perhaps not one pin in a day; that is, certainly, not the two hundred and fortieth, perhaps not the four thousand eight hundredth part of what they are at present capable of performing, in consequence of a proper division and combination of their different operations.

In every other art and manufacture, the effects of the division of labour are similar to what they are in this very trifling one; though, in many of them, the labour can neither be so much subdivided, nor reduced to so great a simplicity of operation. The division of labour, so far as it can be introduced, occasions, in every art, a proportionable increase of the productive powers of labour. The separation of different trades and employments from one another seems to have taken place in consequence of this advantage. This separation, too, is generally called furthest in those countries which enjoy the highest degree of industry and improvement; what is the work of one man in a rude state of society being generally that of several in an improved one.[…]

This great increase of the quantity of work which, in consequence of the division of labour, the same number of people are capable of performing, is owing to three different circumstances; first, to the increase of dexterity in every particular workman; secondly, to the saving of the time which is commonly lost in passing from one species of work to another; and lastly, to the invention of a great number of machines which facilitate and abridge labour, and enable one man to do the work of many. (book I, chapter 1)

http://www.econlib.org/library/Topics/Details/invisible-hand.html

M2 Andrew Ure, The Philosophy of the Manufacturers, 1835

Andrew Ure (1778–1857), taught as a professor at the University of Glasgow and was an enthusiast for the new manufacturing system. Here he represents the views of a new class: the manufacturers whose wealth derived from ownership of factories.

This island is pre-eminent among civilized nations for the prodigious development of its factory wealth, and has been therefore long viewed with a jealous admiration by foreign powers. […] The constant aim and effect of scientific improvement in manufactures are philanthropic, as they tend to relieve the workmen either from niceties of adjustment which exhaust his mind and fatigue his eyes, or from painful repetition of efforts which distort or wear out his frame. […] The principle of the factory system is, to substitute mechanical science for hand skill, and the partition of a process into its essential constituents, for the

division or graduation of labour among artisans. On the handicraft plan, labour more or less skilled was usually the most expensive element of production ... but on the automatic plan, skilled labour gets progressively superseded, and will, eventually, be replaced by mere overlookers of machines.
By the infirmity of human nature it happens, that the more skilful the workman, the more self-willed and intractable he is apt to become, and, of course, the less fit a component of a mechanical system, in which, by occasional irregularities, he may do great damage to the whole. The grand object therefore of the modern manufacturer is, through the union of capital and science, to reduce the task of his work-people to the exercise of vigilance and dexterity, – faculties, when concentred to one process, speedily brought to perfection in the young. [...] It is, in fact, the constant aim and tendency of every improvement in machinery to supersede human labour altogether, or to diminish its cost, by substituting the industry of women and children for that of men; or that of ordinary labourers for trained artisans. In most of the water-twist, or throstle cotton-mills, the spinning is entirely managed by females of sixteen years and upwards. [...]
Steam-engines furnish the means not only of their support but of their multiplication. They create a vast demand for fuel; and, while they lend their powerful arms to drain the pits and to raise the coals, they call into employment multitudes of miners, engineers, shipbuilders, and sailors, and cause the construction of canals and railways. Thus therefore, in enabling these rich fields of industry to be cultivated to the utmost, they leave thousands of fine arable fields free for the production of food to man, which must have been otherwise allotted to the food of horses. Steam-engines moreover, by the cheapness and steadiness of their action, fabricate cheap goods, and procure in their exchange a liberal supply of the necessaries and comforts of life produced in foreign lands.
Improvements in the machinery have a threefold bearing: –
lst. They make it possible to fabricate some articles which, but for them, could not be fabricated at all.
2nd. They enable an operative to turn out a greater quantity of work than he could before, – time, labour, and quality of work remaining constant.
3rd. They effect a substitution of labour comparatively unskilled, for that which is more skilled.

From Andrew Ure, The Philosophy of Manufactures (London: Chas. Knight 1835).

M3 Andrew Carnegie: The Gospel of Wealth, 1889

Andrew Carnegie (1835–1919), a 19th century American steel magnate who left the bulk of his fortune to charity.

What is the proper mode of administering wealth after the laws upon which civilization is founded have thrown it into the hands of the few? [...] There are but three modes in which surplus wealth can be disposed of. It can be left to the families of the decedents; or it can be bequeathed for public purposes; or, finally, it can be administered during their lives by its possessors. [...]
Why should men leave great fortunes to their children? If this is done from affection, is it not misguided affection? Observation teaches that, generally speaking, it is not well for the children that they should be so burdened. Neither is it well for the state. Beyond providing for the wife and daughters moderate sources of income, and very moderate allowances indeed, if any, for the sons, men may well hesitate, for it is no longer questionable that great sums bequeathed oftener work more for the injury than for the good of the recipients. Wise men will soon conclude that, for the best interests of the members of their families and of the state, such bequests are an improper use of their means.
As to the second mode, that of leaving wealth at death for public uses, it may be said that this is only a means for the disposal of wealth, provided a man is content to wait until he is dead before it becomes of much good in the world [...]

There remains, then, only one mode of using great fortunes: but in this way we have the true antidote for the temporary unequal distribution of wealth, the reconciliation of the rich and the poor-a reign of harmony-another ideal, differing, indeed from that of the Communist in requiring only the further evolution of existing conditions, not the total overthrow of our civilization. It is founded upon the present most intense individualism, and the race is prepared to put it in practice by degrees whenever it pleases. Under its sway we shall have an ideal state, in which the surplus wealth of the few will become, in the best sense, the property of the many, because administered for the common good, and this wealth, passing through the hands of the few, can be made a much more potent force for the elevation of our race than if it had been distributed in small sums to the people themselves. Even the poorest can be made to see this, and to agree that great sums gathered by some of their fellowcitizens and spent for public purposes, from which the masses reap the principal benefit, are more valuable to them than if scattered among them through the course of many years in trifling amounts. This, then, is held to be the duty of the man of Wealth: First, to set an example of modest, unostentatious living, shunning display or extravagance; to provide moderately for the legitimate wants of those dependent upon him; and after doing so to consider all surplus revenues which come to him simply as trust funds, which he is called upon to administer, and strictly bound as a matter of duty to administer in the manner which, in his judgment, is best calculated to produce the most beneficial result for the community-the man of wealth thus becoming the sole agent and trustee for his poorer brethren, bringing to their service his superior wisdom, experience, and ability to administer-doing for them better than they would or could do for themselves.

Andrew Carnegie, „Wealth," North American Review, 148, no. 391 (June 1889): 653, 657–62.

M4 The Workers and the Industrial Revolution – an Assessment

Phyllis Deane was an economist at Newnham College, Cambridge University

One of the most persistent controversies in the history of the industrial revolution is the argument that has raged around workers' standard of living. Two schools have grown up in connection with this topic. The pessimistic view, held by a long line of observers from contemporaries of the process to modern historians is that the early stage of industrialization in England, though it brought affluence to some, caused a net deterioration in the standard of living of the labouring poor. The optimistic view, put forward by an equally long list of observers is that although economic change left some workers displaced and distressed, the majority of them were enabled by falling prices, more regular employment and a wider range of earning opportunities to enjoy a rising standard of living.
The controversy has been muddied by political prejudice and the myopic views to which prejudice so often gives rise. It is common to find left-wing writers, their sympathies strongly engaged by the sufferings of the proletariat, holding the pessimistic view; and it equally common to find right-wing writers, more confident of the blessings assured by free capitalistic enterprise, holding the optimistic view. Engels, whose Condition of the Working Class in England (originally published in 1844) is one of the most vivid and angry denunciations of the factory system, makes no bones about his political motives. In a letter written to Karl Marx he called his book a 'bill of indictment'. 'At the bar of world opinion', he wrote, 'I charge the English middle classes with mass murder, wholesale robbery, and all the other crimes in the calendar'. The theory of deterioration was buttressed by a somewhat legendary picture of the golden age that was supposed to have preceded the industrial revolution – an England of happy prosperous yeomen and independent domestic craftsmen free from exploitation and care. [...]

To some extent it is true that there was a shift in the distribution of incomes in favour of profits and rent and a change in the composition of output in favour of capital goods, exports and goods and services for upper-class consumption. But it is manifest that this is not the whole story. The new factories were not producing entirely for the export or the luxury trade or for producers, and the fact that prices of manufactured consumer-goods fell substantially meant that the working classes gained as consumers where they did not gain as wage-earners. So that while on balance the evidence is strongly in favour of the view that working-class standards of living improved by less than the increase in national income per head would suggest over the first half of the nineteenth century; and while there is no doubt that certain sectors of the labouring poor suffered a serious deterioration in their earning-power because they were made redundant by technical progress, nevertheless it would be difficult to credit an overall decline in real incomes per wage-earning family in a period when aggregate real incomes for the nation as a whole were growing appreciably faster than population. In effect, the sustained growth of national product to which industrialization gave rise tended to exert an upward pressure on working-class standards of living in three main ways, none of which implied a rise in the price of labour: (1) by creating more regular employment opportunities for all members of the family – this meant high earnings per year and per family even without a rise in wages per man-hour worked; (2) by creating more opportunities for labour specialization and hence for the higher earnings that semi-skilled or skilled labour can command: here again the average earnings can rise without an increase in the wage rate because the composition of the labour force changes in favour of the higher earning groups; and (3) the upward pressure on the workers' standard of living also operated through the reductions in the prices of consumer goods and the widening of the range of commodities which come within the budget of the working classes. Finally, of course, to the extent that it raised real purchasing power for the masses, industrialization expanded the market for manufactured goods and so justified further increases in investment and output.

Phyllis Deane, The First Industrial Revolution, Cambridge University Press, Cambridge 1965, pp. 238/239 + 252/253.

3. Imperialism

Imperialism – Expansion? Colonialism? New Imperialism? Globalization? The Expansion of human beings beyond their territory is as old as humanity itself. Ever since human beings tried to expand their 'civilization', settle in (or conquer) foreign lands or exploit foreign territories cultures have mingled or even clashed. Sometimes the contact has been friendly and characterized by mutual stimulation, sometimes it has ended in bloodshed and turmoil. Since the 'discovery of the Americas' in the late 15th century this process has become in a manner of speaking truly global as European powers have spread out all over the globe.

After this first global wave of imperialism the major players seemed to have settled with the status quo. The imagination or awareness of the (national) importance of colonies then came to a sudden climax once again in the late 19th century which led to the 'Scramble for Africa' and the 'opening' of China and other Asian countries. New players competed (sometimes successfully) with the 'old imperial powers' and the division of the world came to an abrupt end only when nearly all the countries had been divided by the great European powers. From then on, further expansion was only possible with the highest risk of stepping onto some other power's toes with foreseeable consequences. The many colonial conflicts and crises at the turn of the century showed how dangerously the volatile 'balance of power' had been disturbed, disturbances that would help to ignite World War I. And even during the process of decolonization after World War II imperial endeavors caused a great deal of irritation during the Cold War between the two power blocs, leading close to the brink of another major conflict.

It is impossible to cover the whole history of imperialism in documents. Therefore in the main, only two major strands of imperialism will be followed: the direct rule as it was exercized in India by the British, and secondly the indirect approach which can be exemplified in the imperial politics of the United States of America.

The psychological foundation, the 'imperial mindset' and the historical evaluation of this era – if one can call it an era, as its repercussions can still be felt today, and – some argue – it is far from being over – will touch upon all kinds and events of imperialism, thus ensuring that the following documents can be discussed in various contexts of this all-embracing phenomenon of human history.

Unfortunately, the voice of the colonized is once again drowned out by the voice of the colonizers, which means that it is nearly impossible to obtain any trustworthy source material (in translation) of the colonized people – prior to decolonization. As in many other publications, this small collection must do with the criticism on imperialism that comes from within the colonizing societies themselves.

3.1 Introduction: Controversial Issues

M1 African Proverb

When the whites came to our country, we had the land and they had the Bible, now we have the Bible and they have the land.

http://www.edteck.com/dbq/dbquest/quest10.htm

M2 An Anthology of West African Verse, David Diop, 1957

French born David Diop (1927–1960) became known as a promising French African poet, whose career was cut short by his tragic early death in an airplane crash. His poems voice his angry protest against European oppression through the slave trade and the domination of colonial rule. He opposed any notion that Africa might have gained in any way from the colonial experience.

The White Man killed my father,
My father was proud.
The White Man seduced my mother,
My mother was beautiful.
The White Man burnt my brother beneath the noonday sun,
My brother was strong.
His hands red with black blood
The White Man turned to me;
And in the Conqueror's voice said,
"Boy! a chair, a napkin, a drink."

Bassir, Olumbe (Hrsg.): An Anthology of West African Verse. Ibadan: University Press 1957.
Online: http://www.edteck.com/dbq/dbquest/quest10.htm

M3 Ahmed Sékou Touré, West African Nationalist, 1962

Ahmed Sékou Touré was a West African nationalist, who led Guinea into independence from France and was elected Guinea's president in 1958.

Colonialism's greatest misdeed was to have tried to strip us of our responsibility in conducting our own affairs and convince us that our civilization was nothing less than savagery, thus giving us complexes which led to our being branded as irresponsible and lacking in self-confidence […]

The colonial powers had assimilated each of their colonies into their own economy.
Our continent possesses tremendous reserves of raw material and they, together with its potential sources of power, give it excellent conditions for industrialization […]

http://www.edteck.com/dbq/dbquest/quest10.htm

M4 Hans Kohn: The Meaning of Imperialism, Colonialism and their Variations, 1958

The meaning and implications of the word "colonialism", and of the closely connected terms "empire" and "imperialism," have undergone a profound transformation in recent decades. Until the end of the nineteenth century the words "empire" and "imperialism" were generally used in a laudatory and not a pejorative sense. The Roman empire had been the model for Western political thought for over a thousand years. Americans at the end of the eighteenth century spoke proudly and hopefully of their "empire." The French revolutionaries proclaimed the "imperial" expansion of their leadership. Modern Western civilization was regarded as superior to other, comparatively stagnant civilizations, and to bring higher civilization to less developed countries was considered a praiseworthy enterprise, in spite of the fact that like so many other human efforts this, too, was inextricably mingled with corruption and greed. […]
Not every "imperial" relationship is "colonial." On the contrary, indeed, the colonial relationship has generally been the exceptional result of conquest; at least it was until the fifteenth century "age of discoveries." When a nation expands by annexing contiguous territory, it has roughly five alternatives, which may in practice shade imperceptibly into one another. It may – though it rarely does – accord the subject people full autonomy within an imperial framework, as Austria did with Hungary, and as Russia pretended to do with Georgia and the Ukraine, and actually did do for a time after acquiring Finland in 1809. It

may – at the other extreme – annihilate or expel the inhabitants and settle the area as an integral part of itself, as the Americans did with most of the United States and the Russians with much of Siberia. Or it may, less drastically, permit the indigenes to remain, but in a permanently inferior status, as in the caste-ridden India or the virulently racist Union of South Africa. Or it may accord full citizenship to the individuals of the subject nation, and attempt to submerge their nationhood in a larger nation, as Turkey has done with the Kurds, Italy with the South Tyroleans, Great Britain with the Welsh, New Zealand with the Maoris, and Pakistan with the Bengalis; this has been the commonest of the four imperial but non-colonial solutions.

The fifth alternative, often applied to contiguous territories and almost invariably to overseas or other noncontiguous acquisitions, has been colonialism. A colonial relationship is created when one nation establishes and maintains political domination over a geographically external political unit inhabited by people of any race and at any stage of cultural development. It is terminated whenever the subject people becomes fully self-governing as an autonomous state, whether independent or as a voluntary associate within an imperial or commonwealth partnership from which it may withdraw at will. It is also terminated whenever a subject people becomes assimilated into the political structure of the colonial power on equal terms, or when their political unit is thus assimilated [...]

American thinking about colonialism has been largely influenced by emotional misunderstandings. For obvious reasons, the United States from the outset insisted on striving for complete political, economic, cultural, and ideological independence from Great Britain, disregarding the interdependence and affinity existing in all these respects between two nations which had developed from the same historical roots. The striving for independence led inescapably to competition and to overcompensation for the then existing cultural and political inferiorities by the assumption of a posture of moral superiority.

In addition to this emotional bias, there existed the widespread though unwarranted assumption [...] that colonial "empires" are established by sea powers, whereas expansion into contiguous land masses does not produce "empires" or colonialism. The agrarian empire of Rome had looked with contempt upon Carthage's maritime empire, but Rome was an empire too. And the United States in its war against Mexico and in its many wars against the various Indian tribes created as real an empire as did the seafaring island states of Great Britain and Japan. Yet the United States, considering itself not an "imperial" power [...] applied similar criteria of nonimperialism to the military conquests and ruthless expansive policies of Russia and China. These land empires were never regarded in the same way as were the sea empires. [...]

Western imperialism has had only a brief day in history. Its sun is now setting, and though this sun has shone over many injustices and cruelties – though these were in no way worse than the normal cruelties in Asia and Africa – it has brought lasting benefits to both continents, as the imperialism of Alexander the Great and of the Romans did to their empires, and has awakened and vitalized lethargic civilizations.

Now the tide of Western imperialism is definitely receding, due to so much to external pressure as to Western ideas themselves – but it has been on the whole a period of which the West and especially Great Britain has no need to be ashamed. It would be a mistake to apply twentieth-century ethical standards and principles of international law to preceding centuries. By doing exactly that – and it should not be forgotten that these new altruistic twentieth-century standards were developed by the Western world and only by the Western world – the West suffers from an unnecessarily bad conscience [...]

Snyder, Louis L. (Hrsg.): The Imperialism Reader. Documents and Readings on Modern Expansionism. Princeton (u. a.): D. van Nostrand Company New Jersey 1962, S. 44–51.

M5 Monroe Doctrine

From President James Monroe's seventh annual message to Congress, December 2, 1823:

At the proposal of the Russian Imperial Government, made through the minister of the Emperor residing here, a full power and instructions have been transmitted to the Minister of the United States at St. Petersburg to arrange, by amicable negotiation, the respective rights and interests of the two nations on the northwest coast of this continent. A similar proposal has been made by His Imperial Majesty to the Government of Great Britain, which has likewise been acceded to. The Government of the United States has been desirous, by this friendly proceeding, of manifesting the great value which they have invariably attached to the friendship of the Emperor, and their solicitude to cultivate the best understanding with his Government. In the discussions to which this interest has given rise, and in the arrangements by which they may terminate the occasion has been judged proper for asserting, as a principle in which the rights and interests of the United States are involved, that the American continents, by the free and independent condition which they have assumed and maintain, are henceforth not to be considered as subjects for future colonization by any European powers. [...]

In the wars of the European powers, in matters relating to themselves, we have never taken any part, nor does it comport with our policy to do so. It is only when our rights are invaded, or seriously menaced, that we resent injuries, or make preparation for our defence. With the movements in this hemisphere, we are, of necessity, more immediately connected, and by causes which must be obvious to all enlightened and impartial observers. The political system of the allied powers is essentially different, in this respect, from that of America. This difference proceeds from that which exists in their respective governments. And to the defence of our own, which has been achieved by the loss of so much blood and treasure, and matured by the wisdom of their most enlightened citizens, and under which we have enjoyed unexampled felicity, this whole nation is devoted. We owe it, therefore, to candor, and to the amicable relations existing between the United States and those powers, to declare, that we should consider any attempt on their part to extend their system to any portion of this hemisphere, as dangerous to our peace and safety. With the existing colonies or dependencies of any European power we have not interfered, and shall not interfere. But with the governments who have declared their independence, and maintained it, and whose independence we have, on great consideration, and on just principles, acknowledged, we could not view any interposition for the purpose of oppressing them, or controlling, in any other manner, their destiny, by any European power in any other light than as the manifestation of an unfriendly disposition towards the United States. [...]

Elliot, Ian (Hrsg.): James Monroe, 1758–1831: Chronology – Documents – Bibliographical Aids. Dobbs Ferry (USA): Oceana Publications 1969, S. 68 f.
Online: http://www.ushistory.org/documents/monroe.htm

3.2 Legitimation

M1 Count de Gobineau on the "Inequality of Human Races"

Joseph-Arthur Comte de Gobineau (1816–1882) was a French diplomat, writer, ethnologist, and social thinker whose theory of racial determinism had an enormous influence upon the subsequent development of racist theories and practices in western Europe. His "Essai sur l'inégalité des races humaines" ("Essays on the Inequality of Human Races", 4 vol. 1853–1855), was by far his most influential work. Gobineau's theories, now discredited, were the product of years of historical, anthropological, and ethnological studies and were part of a general European interest in biological and sociological determinism.

I have been able to distinguish on physiological grounds alone, three great and clearly marked types, the black, the yellow, and the white [...]

The negroid variety is the lowest, and stands at the foot of the ladder. The animal character, that appears in the shape of the pelvis, is stamped on the negro from birth, and foreshadows his destiny. His intellect will always move within a very narrow circle. He is not however a mere brute, for behind his low receding brow, in the middle of his skull, we can see signs of a powerful energy, however crude its objects. If his mental faculties are dull or even non-existent, he often has an intensity of desire and so of will, which may be called terrible. Many of his senses, especially taste and smell, are developed to an extent unknown to the other two races.

The very strength of his sensations is the most striking proof of his inferiority. All food is good in his eyes, nothing disgusts or repels him [...] It is the same with odours; his inordinate desires are satisfied with all, however coarse or even horrible. To these qualities may be added an instability and capriciousness of feeling that cannot be tied down to any single object, and which, so far as he is concerned, do away with all distinctions of good and evil. We might even say that the violence with which he pursues the object that has aroused his senses and inflamed his desires is a guarantee of the desires being soon satisfied and the object forgotten [...]

The yellow race is the exact opposite of this type. The skull points forward, not backward. The forehead is wide and bony, often high and projecting. The shape of the face is triangular, the nose and chin showing none of the coarse protuberances that mark the negro. There is further a general proneness to obesity, which, though not confined to the yellow type, is found there more frequently than in the others. The yellow man has little physical energy, and is inclined to apathy, he commits none of the strange excess so common among negroes. His desires are feeble, his will-power rather obstinate than violent; his longing for material pleasures, though constant, is kept within bounds. A rare glutton by nature, he shows more discrimination in his choice of food. He tends to mediocrity in everything; he understands easily enough anything not too deep or sublime. He has a love of utility and a respect for order, and knows the value of a certain amount of freedom. He is practical, in the narrowest sense of the word, he does not dream or theorize, he invents little [...]

We come now to the white peoples. These are gifted with reflective energy, or rather with an energetic intelligence. They have a feeling for utility, but in a sense far wider and higher, more courageous and ideal, than the yellow races; a perseverance that takes account of obstacles and ultimately finds a means of over-coming them; a greater physical power, an extraordinary instinct for order, not merely as a guarantee of peace and tranquility, but as an indispensable means of self-preservation. At the same time, they have a remarkable, and even extreme, love of liberty, and are openly hostile to the formalism under which the Chinese are glad to vegetate, as well as to the strict despotism which is the only way of governing the negro.

Such is the lesson of history. It shows us that all civilizations derive from the white race, that none can exist without its help and that a society is great and brilliant only so far as it preserves the blood of the noble group that created it, provided that this group itself belongs to the most illustrious branch of our species.

Smith, Bonnie G.: Imperialism. A History in Documents. Oxford 2000, S. 96–97.

M2 Rudyard Kipling: The White Man's Burden

Rudyard Kipling (British novelist and poet, 1865–1936, most famous for his Jungle Books) wrote the following poem in light of the American-Spanish War, by which the U.S. had taken control of the Philippines. Kipling urges the U.S. to take up their colonial duties as the European colonial empires had done before; the poem became rather famous, not so much because of its artistic merit but as a clear expression of imperial contemporary thought. Its sentiments were picked up in advertisements and its imperial message was ridiculed by anti-imperialists.

Take up the White Man's burden--
Send forth the best ye breed--
Go bind your sons to exile
To serve your captives' need;
To wait in heavy harness,
On fluttered folk and wild--
Your new-caught, sullen peoples,
Half-devil and half-child.

Take up the White Man's burden--
In patience to abide,
To veil the threat of terror
And check the show of pride;
By open speech and simple,
A hundred times made plain
To seek another's profit,
And work another's gain.

Take up the White Man's burden--
The savage wars of peace--
Fill full the mouth of Famine
And bid the sickness cease;
And when your goal is nearest
The end for others sought,
Watch sloth and heathen Folly
Bring all your hopes to nought. [...]

Take up the White Man's burden--
And reap his old reward:
The blame of those ye better,
The hate of those ye guard--
The cry of hosts ye humour
(Ah, slowly!) toward the light:--
"Why brought he us from bondage,
Our loved Egyptian night?" [...]

Kipling, Rudyard: The complete Verse. London: Cathie 1990, S. 261 f.

M3 Joseph Chamberlain on Imperialism, Birmingham 1893

Joseph Chamberlain (1836–1914), was a very able and successful businessman, which allowed him to 'retire' from his Birmingham factory at the age of 38 and turn to politics. Held a speech in front of Birmingham's businessmen in 1893, in which his strong pro imperialism views are easy to discern:

We must look this matter in the face, and must recognize that in order that we may have more employment to give we must create more demand [*hear, hear*]. Give me the demand for more goods and then I will undertake to give plenty of employment in making the goods; and the only thing, in my opinion, that the government can do in order to meet this great difficulty that we are considering, is to arrange its policy that every inducement shall be given to the demand; that new markets shall be created, and that old markets shall be effectually developed [*cheers*].
You are aware that some of my opponents please themselves occasionally by finding names for me, and among other names lately they have been calling me a Jingo [laughter]. I am no more a Jingo than you are [*hear, hear*]. But for the reasons and arguments I have put before you tonight I am convinced that it is a necessity as well as a duty for us to uphold the dominion and empire which we now possess [*loud cheers*]. For these reasons, among others, I would never lose the hold which we now have over our great Indian dependency [*hear, hear*], by far the greatest and most valuable of all the customers we have or ever shall have in this country. For the same reasons I approve of the continued occupation of Egypt, and for the same reasons I have urged upon this government, and upon previous governments, the necessity for using every legitimate opportunity to extend our influence and control in that great African continent which is now being opened up to civilization and commerce; and, lastly, it is for the same reasons that I hold that our navy should be strengthened [*loud cheers*] until its supremacy is so assured that we cannot be shaken

in any of the possessions which we hold or may hold hereafter.

Believe me, if in any one of the places to which I have referred any change took place which deprived us of the control and influence of which I have been speaking, the first to suffer would be the workingman of this country. Then, indeed, we should see a distress which would not be temporary, but which would be chronic, and we should find that England was entirely unable to support the enormous population which is now maintained by the aid of her foreign trade. [...] If the 'Little Englanders" had their way, not only would they refrain from taking the legitimate opportunities which offer for extending the empire and for securing for us new markets, but I doubt whether they would even take the pains which are necessary to preserve the great heritage which has come down to us from our ancestors [*applause*].

M4 The White Man's Burden (by William H. Walker), *Live* (March 16, 1899)

When you are told that the British pioneers of civilization in Africa are filibusters, and when you are asked to call them back, and to leave this great continent to the barbarism and superstition in which it has been steeped for centuries, or to hand over to foreign countries the duty which you are unwilling to undertake, I ask you to consider what would have happened if, one hundred and fifty years ago, our ancestors had taken similar views of their responsibility? Where would be the empire on which now your livelihood depends? We should have been the United Kingdom of Great Britain and Ireland, but those vast dependencies, those hundreds of millions with whom we keep up a mutually beneficial relationship and commerce would have been the subjects of other nations, who would not have been slow to profit by our neglect of opportunities and obligations [*applause*]. […]

Snyder, Louis L. (Hrsg.): The Imperialism Reader. Documents and Readings on Modern Expansionism. Princeton (u.a.): D. van Nostrad Company 1962, S. 125 f.

3.3 Profit and Loss

M1 Sir Henry Parnell's Cost-Benefit Analysis

Sir Henry Brooke Parnell (Baron Congleton, 1776–1842), an Anglo-Irish politician, in his "On Financial Reform" (1830) makes a less enthusiastic cost-benefit analysis:

There are only three ways that the colonies can be of any advantage, 1. In furnishing a military force; 2. In supplying the parent state with a revenue; 3. In affording commercial advantages.

1. Instead of furnishing a military force, the colonies are always a drain upon the military resources of the country, particularly in war, when they occupy a large portion of the army and fleet in their defence. In the last war, while our own shores were threatened with invasion from Boulogne and Brest, our means of defence were greatly crippled by the number of troops and ships we were obliged to keep in the colonies.

2. With respect to revenue, we have declared […], that we will not levy any taxes or duties in the colonies except for their use.

3. As to commercial advantages, if the colonial trade were quite free, our commercial relations with the colonies would resemble the intercourse between ourselves and independent countries; and therefore whatever advantages we shall derive from them will be embraced in two questions: 1st. Whether our commerce with them will be more beneficial than with independent countries? 2nd. Whether the capital employed in them will be more beneficially employed than it would be, if employed in the United Kingdom?

With respect to the first question, it is one easily solved, because, where the employment of capital is free, the net profit that may be obtained by the employment of it in commerce with independent countries will always be as great as if it were employed in the colonial trade. The trade we carry on with the United States proves this.

With respect to the second question, it is necessary to trace the operations of capital when employed in colonies, and when employed at home. In the West India islands it goes to feed and clothe slaves; to pay British agents, clerks, and managers; to employ ships and sailors; and although the gross profit upon it seems very high when all the charges and risks are considered, and also the effects of competition, the net profit cannot be greater than it is on capital employed at home.

When capital is employed in the United Kingdom – for instance, on manufactures – it pays wages to English workmen instead of buying clothes and food for slaves; it employs agents, clerks, and managers; it employs ships and sailors to import raw materials and to export the finished goods, and the rate of net profit on it is fully as high as that on capital employed in the colonies. The incomes derived by West India proprietors from their profits are spent like incomes derived from rent, and add

nothing to the national wealth; but the profits made on capital employed at home are added to capital, and thus promote the constant accumulation of it. It is clear, therefore, that, on the whole, the public derives no commercial advantage from the colonies, which it might not have without them. [...]
This general reasoning, which the principles of trade suggest, in refutation of the imaginary advantages of colonies, is completely borne out by the experience of facts. The history of the colonies for many years is that of a series of loss, and of the destruction of capital; and if to the many millions of private capital, which have been thus wasted, were added some hundred millions that have been raised by British taxes and spent on account of the colonies, the total loss to the British public of wealth, which the colonies have occasioned, would appear to be quite enormous. [...]

Snyder, Louis L. (Hrsg.): The Imperialism Reader. Documents and Readings on Modern Expansionism. Princeton (u.a.): D. van Nostrad Company 1962, S. 145–147.

M2 John A. Hobson: Imperialism

John Atkinson Hobson (1858–1940, British economist) in his influential study on imperialism considers the underlying motivation of imperialism and who benefits most by it. His ideas later influenced Marxist thinkers such as Lenin.

Seeing that the Imperialism of the last three decades is clearly condemned as a business policy, in that at enormous expense it has procured a small, bad, unsafe increase of markets, and has jeopardised the entire wealth of the nation in rousing the strong resentment of other nations, we may ask, "How is the British nation induced to embark upon such unsound business?" The only possible answer is that the business interests of the nation as a whole are subordinated to those of certain sectional interests that usurp control of the national resources and use them for their private gain. This is no strange or monstrous charge to bring; it is the commonest disease of all forms of government. The famous words of Sir Thomas More are as true now as when he wrote them: "Everywhere do I perceive a certain conspiracy of rich men seeking their own advantage under the name and pretext of the commonwealth."
Although the new Imperialism has been bad business for the nation, it has been good business for certain classes and certain trades within the nation. The vast expenditure on armaments, the costly wars, the grave risks and embarrassments of foreign policy, the stoppage of political and social reforms within Great Britain, though fraught with great injury to the nation, have served well the present business interests of certain industries and professions. [...]
What is the direct economic outcome of Imperialism? A great expenditure of public money upon ships, guns, military and naval equipment and stores, growing and productive of enormous profits when a war, or an alarm of war, occurs; new public loans and important fluctuations in the home and foreign Bourses; more posts for soldiers and sailors and in the diplomatic and consular services; improvement of foreign investments by the substitution of the British flag for a foreign flag; acquisition of markets for certain classes of exports, and some protection and assistance for trades representing British houses in these manufactures; employment for engineers, missionaries, speculative miners, ranchers and other emigrants.
Aggressive Imperialism, which costs the taxpayer so dear, which is of so little value to the manufacturer and trader, which is fraught with such grave incalculable peril to the citizen, is a source of great gain to the investor who cannot find at home the profitable use he seeks for his capital, and insists that his Government should help him to profitable and secure investments abroad.
If, contemplating the enormous expenditure on armaments, the ruinous wars, the diplomatic audacity of knavery by which modern Governments seek to extend their territorial power, we put the plain, practical question, *Cui bono*? the first and most obvious answer is, The investor. [...]

Investors who have put their money in foreign lands, upon terms which take full account of risks connected with the political conditions of the country, desire to use the resources of their Government to minimise these risks, and so to enhance the capital value and the interest of their private investments. The investing and speculative classes in general also desire that Great Britain should take other foreign areas under her flag in order to secure new areas for profitable investment and speculation. [...]

In view of the part which the non-economic factors of patriotism, adventure, military enterprise, political ambition, and philanthropy play in imperial expansion, it may appear that to impute to financiers so much power is to take a too narrowly economic view of history. And it is true that the motor-power of Imperialism is not chiefly financial: finance is rather the governor of the imperial engine, directing the energy and determining its work: it does not constitute the fuel of the engine, nor does it directly generate the power. Finance manipulates the patriotic forces which politicians, soldiers, philanthropists, and traders generate; the enthusiasm for expansion which issues from these sources, though strong and genuine, is irregular and blind; the financial interest has those qualities of concentration and clear-sighted calculation which are needed to set Imperialism to work. An ambitious statesman, a frontier soldier, an overzealous missionary, a pushing trader, may suggest or even initiate a step of imperial expansion, may assist in educating patriotic public opinion to the urgent need of some fresh advance, but the final determination rests with the financial power. The direct influence exercised by great financial houses in "high politics" is supported by the control which they exercise over the body of public opinion through the Press, which, in every "civilised" country, is becoming more and more their obedient instrument. While the specifically financial newspaper imposes "facts" and "opinions" on the business classes, the general body of the Press comes more and more under the conscious or unconscious domination of financiers. [...]

Such is the array of distinctively economic forces making for Imperialism, a large loose group of trades and professions seeking profitable business and lucrative employment from the expansion of military and civil services, from the expenditure on military operations, the opening up of new tracts of territory and trade with the same, and the provision of new capital which these operations require, all these finding their central guiding and directing force in the power of the general financier.

The play of these forces does not openly appear. They are essentially parasites upon patriotism, and they adapt themselves to its protecting colours. In the mouths of their representatives are noble phrase, expressive of their desire to extend the area of civilisation, to establish good government, promote Christianity, extirpate slavery, and elevate the lower races. Some of the business men who hold such language may entertain a genuine, though usually a vague, desire to accomplish these ends, but they are primarily engaged in business, and they are not unaware of the utility of the more unselfish forces in furthering their ends. Their true attitude of mind is expressed by Mr. Rhodes in his famous description of "Her Majesty's Flag" as "the greatest commercial asset in the world."

Hobson, John A.: Imperialism. A Study. New York: James Pott & Company 1902, S. 51–68.

3.4 Acquisition

M1 The Flag follows the Trade? One Example of 'Acquisition'

Cecil Rhodes Obtains a Concession in Southern Rhodesia from Lo Bengula.

Cecil Rhodes (1853–1902), most likely the most famous British imperialist, was one of the 'men on the spot', adventurers who 'acquired land or rights to exploit the natural resources from the local rulers, used these as the basis to form companies (e.g. the British South Africa Company) and called in their home governments for protection if met by resistance. The following documents show, in what way men like Rhodes obtained their goals. This treaty formed the basis of the following concession, which became one of the main sources for Rhodes' wealth:

a) The Concession

Know all men by these presents, that whereas Charles Dunell Rudd, of Kimberley; Rochfort Maguire, of London; and Francis Robert Thompson, of Kimberley, have covenanted and agreed [...] to pay me [...] the sum of one hundred pounds sterling, British currency, on the first day of every lunar month; and further, to deliver at my royal kraal one thousand Martini-Henry breech-loading rifles, together with one hundred thousand rounds of suitable ball cartridges [...] and further to deliver on the Zambesi River a steamboat with guns suitable for defensive purposes, or in lieu of the said steamboat, should I elect, to pay to me the Sufi of five hundred pounds sterling, British currency. On the execution of these presents, I, Lo Bengula, King of Matabeleland, Mashonaland, and other adjoining territories [...] do hereby grant and assign unto the said grantees [...] the complete and exclusive charge over all metals and minerals situated and contained in my kingdoms [...] together with full power to do all things that they may deem necessary to win and procure the same, and to hold, collect, and enjoy the profits and revenues, if any, derivable from the said metals and minerals, subject to the aforesaid payment; and [...] I do hereby authorize the said grantees [...] to exclude from my kingdom [...] all persons seeking land, metals, minerals, or mining rights therein, and I do hereby undertake to render them all such needful assistance as they may from time to time require for the exclusion of such persons, and to grant no concessions of land or mining rights [...] without their consent and concurrence [...]. This given under my hand this thirtieth day of October, in the year of Our Lord 1888, at my royal kraal.

Lo Bengula X his mark C. D. Rudd Rochfort Maguire F. R. Thompson

Snyder, Louis L. (Hrsg.): The Imperialism Reader. Documents and Readings on Modern Expansionism. Princeton (u.a.): D. van Nostrad Company 1962, S. 219–22.

b) The British Position

Shortly after Lo Bengula affixed his seal to the Rudd concession, his people became convinced that their ruler had been induced unfairly to part with their rights. Lo Bengula, after having his fears confirmed by friendly British missionaries, executed his Head Counselor and sent a mission to Queen Victoria. The British Secretary answered in the Queen's name on March 26, 1889:

Lo Bengula is the ruler of his country and the Queen does not interfere in the government of that country. But as Lo Bengula desires her advice Her Majesty is ready to give it [...]. In the first place the Queen wishes Lo Bengula to understand distinctly that Englishmen who have gone to Matabeleland to ask leave to dig for stones have not gone with the Queen's authority and that he should not believe any statement made by them or any of them to that effect. The Queen advises Lo Bengula not to grant hastily concessions of land or leave to dig but to consider all applications very carefully.

c) Lo Bengula protests to Queen Victoria, April 23, 1889

The following appeal from the untutored African ruler, apparently a victim of trickery, had no effect on the course of events. He was later told by the Queen's Advisor that the

Queen had made inquiries as to the persons concerned and was satisfied that they "may be trusted to carry out the working for gold in the chief's country without molesting his people, or in any way interfering with their kraals (villages), gardens (cultivated fields), or cattle." It is interesting to note, that Queen Victoria knew Rhodes personally.

Some time ago a party of men came to my country, the principal one appearing to be a man called Rudd. They asked me for a place to dig for gold, and said they would give me certain things for the right to do so. I told them to bring what they could give and I would show them what I would give. A document was written and presented to me for signature. I asked what it contained, and was told that in it were my words and the words of those men. I put my hand to it. About three months afterwards I heard from other sources that I had given by that document the right to all the minerals of my country. I called a meeting of my Indunas [counselors] , and also of the white men and demanded a copy of the document. It was proved to me that I had signed away the mineral rights of my whole country to Rudd and his friends. I have since had a meeting of my Indunas and they will not recognise the paper, as it contains neither my words nor the words of those who got it [...] I write to you that you may know the truth about this thing.

Snyder, Louis L. (Hrsg.): The Imperialism Reader. Documents and Readings on Modern Expansionism. Princeton (u.a.): D. van Nostrad Company 1962, S. 219–222.

3.5 Case Study: India

M1 British Rule in India in a Contemporary American History Textbook, 2001

"A lucky adventure, a lucky venture!" exclaimed a Muslim trader when Portuguese captain Vasco da Gama reached India in 1498. "Plenty of rubies, plenty of emeralds. You owe great thanks to God for having brought you to a country of such riches."

The Portuguese were the first Europeans to gain a foothold in India. The Dutch, French, and British soon followed. They were eager for a share of the rich Indian trade. At first, the mighty Mughal emperors kept tight control of European activity. In time, however, Mughal power declined. The British, who had come as traders, then turned their attention to conquest.

Mughal Emperors and European Traders

After da Gama's voyage, the Portuguese quickly built a trading empire in Asia. They set up trading posts, from Goa on India's west coast to Southeast Asia. Catholic missionaries sailed with Portuguese merchants and converted many Indians to Christianity.

In the 1600s, the Dutch broke into the Portuguese trade monopoly in Asia. A monopoly is complete control over a market or a product. The English and French also sought trading rights from the Mughals.

Early trade.

In 1600, England set up the East India Company. From the Mughal rulers, the East India Company won rights to build trading posts and forts at Madras, Bombay, and Calcutta. [...] The English traded gold and silver for Indian goods such as cotton, silk, and tea. Textiles, or cloth, were the most important goods carried to England by the East India Company. The influence of this trade can still be seen today, in the Indian words that have entered the English language. They include the words calico, dungarees, gingham, khaki, madras, and shawl.

A struggle for power.

At first, the powerful Mughal rulers looked down on the Europeans. To the Indians, with their rich spices and silks, the newcomers had little of value to offer. The Mughals set the terms of trade and had the power to enforce them.

In the early 1700s, however, changes occurred in India and in Europe that would have major effects on South Asia. In India, the Mughal Empire entered its long period of decline. Emperors still ruled over a rich court, but they no longer controlled most of the subcontinent. Rival princes set up their own, almost independent kingdoms. In Europe, the British and French were competing for political and economic power. This power struggle spilled over into other parts of the world, including India.

The British and French took advantage of the Mughal decline. They competed to control India's many small kingdoms and tap new sources of wealth. Fierce fighting broke out between the two European powers. In their bitter struggle, both sides found allies among local Indian rulers. By the 1760s, however, British forces had overcome the French.

East India Company Rule

Britain owed its success in India in part to Robert Clive, an administrator of the East India Company. Clive led British forces in their successful drive against the French. He also won control of the wealthy Indian state of Bengal. In Bengal and elsewhere, he appointed local rulers who favored the interests of the East India Company.

Many individual Indian rulers fought to keep the British out of their territory. Additional rivalries, however, kept them from uniting. The British encouraged this disunity. The East India Company forced Indian rulers, one by one, to sign treaties granting it greater power.

The East India Company gained enormous wealth from India, especially after the Mughal emperor gave it the right to collect taxes. To protect its interests, the company set up a law code and a court system. It also took over more land. Some areas it ruled directly. Others, it ruled indirectly through local princes.

British Rule

The British government took steps to check the increasing power of the East India Company. Parliament passed laws to regulate affairs. London, however, was far off, and communications were slow.

By the 1850s, Indians had many grievances against British rule. Hindus were outraged when the British outlawed ritual suicide by widows and other Hindu practices. Indian princes disliked having foreigners tell them what to do. High taxes angered farmers. Both Hindus and Muslims resented the efforts of missionaries to convert them to the Christian religion. For many Indians, foreigners were a threat to their whole way of life.

The Sepoy Rebellion.

The general unrest helped spark a revolt among the sepoys, Indian troops who served in the British army. In the 1850s, sepoys heard rumors that the cartridges for their new rifles were greased with beef or pork fat. To Hindus, cows were sacred, and Muslims were forbidden to touch pork. A new law further upset the sepoys. The law required them to fight for Britain in foreign lands. Hindus believed that they would lose caste if they traveled overseas.

The Sepoy Rebellion broke out in 1857 near Delhi. It quickly spread across northern and central India. During several months of fighting, both sides committed savage acts. In the end, the British put down the uprising.

A British colony.

The rebellion led to a number of political changes. In 1858, the British government took over India as a colony. They sent the last Mughal emperor into exile. In 1876, Queen Victoria of Britain took the title Empress of India. The British ruled most of India directly, through appointed officials. About a third of the subcontinent remained in the hands of local rulers. Hindu and Muslim princes governed their own kingdoms but had to sign treaties giving the British control of their foreign and military affairs. The British reformed the law codes and controlled the court system.

The Sepoy Rebellion left lasting distrust between Indians and British. The British moved away from using Indian soldiers and set up their own civil service, or body of officials, to rule the colony. At the same time, they set out to create a new class of British-educated Indians.

Indians continued to resent efforts to change their culture. One Indian commented about widespread racism under British rule:

"In India, every European is automatically a member of the ruling race. Railway carriages, station waiting rooms, benches in parks are marked 'For Europeans Only.' To have to put up with this in one's own country is a humiliating reminder of our enslaved condition."

Effects of British Rule

British rule brought economic and social changes to South Asia. The British improved roads and modernized ports. They directed the building of railroads and telegraph systems. These modern forms of transportation and communications helped the British increase trade and control their colony. Officials could report uprisings or disasters instantly and send troops by rail to trouble spots. Improved communications also brought Indians in different regions closer together.

New economic patterns.

Other changes helped to destroy the traditional Indian economy and tie India economically to Britain. By the mid-1800s, the Industrial Revolution was in full swing in Britain. British factory owners saw India as a market for their own goods. They discouraged local Indian industries and pushed for laws to limit British imports of Indian-made goods. As a result, Indian industries declined, locally made goods disappeared, and Indians had to buy expensive British-made products.

To pay for British imports, Indians had to raise cash crops such as tea, pepper, coffee, and cotton. As Indian farmers grew less food, famines became frequent and widespread. When food shortages occurred, however, rail links allowed officials to send supplies to hard-hit areas.

Social changes.

Britain also introduced changes that affected Indian society. Improved health care and sanitary conditions led to population growth. Many young Indians moved to cities to find jobs.

The British set up schools and colleges to educate higher-caste Indians. The course of study, which stressed English language and culture, reflected British ethnocentrism. To the British, their culture was superior to that of India. As one official boasted, the British wanted to create "a class of persons, Indian in blood and color, but English in taste, in opinions, in morals, and in intellect."

A British-educated Indian middle class emerged. For them, English became a useful common language. Hindi-speakers from the north, for example, could communicate with Tamil-speakers in the south. In studying English history, young Indians learned about political ideals such as liberty, freedom, and "rule by the consent of the governed." Educated Indians also learned more about their own cultural traditions. This awareness increased their resentment against foreign rule and contributed to the growth of nationalism.

Indian Nationalism

Indian nationalism was strongest among the British-educated elite. These people came mostly from the upper and middle classes, and they were determined to change India. At first, nationalists disagreed among themselves about what direction to take. Some wanted to adopt western ways. They wanted to modernize India and reform the system of British rule.

Other nationalists favored a return to Hindu traditions. They wanted to build a new India that blended the best of both Hindu and western cultures. Hindu nationalists won support among poor peasants and other working people. In time, they rejected foreign rule completely and demanded independence.

Indians formed various groups to work for change. Among the most successful was the Indian National Congress (INC), set up in 1885. Most Congress members were Hindus who lived in the cities. The INC began by calling for gradual change. At the same time, it urged the British to open more government jobs to Indians.

After World War I, however, the INC took a more forceful stand. In 1920, Mohandas Gandhi took over the leadership of the Congress movement. [...] he united large sections of the Indian people in support of home rule. Under pressure, Britain promised self-government to India in time. It slowly turned over control

of some areas to local government but kept overall power in the country.
As Hindu nationalism grew, Muslims became concerned. In 1906, they founded the Muslim League under the leadership of Muhammad Ali Jinnah. Tensions and distrust kept Hindus and Muslims apart. By the 1930s, Jinnah came to believe that the subcontinent must be divided into two separate nations – one for Hindus and one for Muslims.

Ahmad, Iftikhar, Brodsky, Herbert; Crofts, Marylee Susan; Ellis, Elisabeth Gaynor: World Cultures. A Global Mosaic. New Jersey 2001, S. 193–198.

3.6 Case Study: USA

M1 "Dollar Imperialism"?

An American history textbook on the relationship between the U.S. and Latin America, 2001

When the nations of Latin America won their freedom, they looked to the United States as a model for democratic government. Simon Bolivar called the United States a "model of political virtues and moral enlightenment unique in the history of mankind." Yet, by the early 1900s, Latin American admiration for the United States had turned to resentment. To many Latin Americans, the United States had become the "Colossus of the North"-a giant power that threatened their independence.

An Expanding Power

In the 1820s, Spain prepared to reconquer its former American colonies. The new nations of Latin America therefore welcomed the Monroe Doctrine, issued by United States President James Monroe in 1823. In it, Monroe declared that "the American continents are henceforth not to be considered as subjects for future colonization by any European powers."

As the United States expanded, Latin Americans no longer saw the United States as a defender of their liberties. Instead, they began to fear its power in the hemisphere.

Mexican War.

In 1845, the United States annexed Texas, which had once belonged to Mexico. A year later, war broke out between Mexico and the United States. When the Mexican War ended in 1848, Mexico had to give up almost half of its territory to the United States. The war left Mexicans with a lasting bitterness toward the United States.

Spanish-American War.

As the United States industrialized, it extended its influence in the Caribbean and Central America. During the 1890s, Cuban patriots were battling for independence from Spain. Many Latin Americans felt that the United States had fought the Spanish-American War to win new territories..

"Yankee Imperialist" or Good Neighbor?

During the early 1900s, the United States continued to intervene in Latin America. Its actions increased Latin Americans' distrust and fear of their northern neighbor.

Panama Canal.

From the late 1800s, the United States had expressed an interest in digging a canal across Panama, which was then part of Colombia. President Theodore Roosevelt offered Colombia $10 million for a strip of land across the Isthmus of Panama. When Colombia rejected the offer, Roosevelt encouraged rebels in Panama to declare Panama's independence. In 1903, the new nation of Panama granted a 100mile-wide "canal zone" to the United States. Roosevelt's actions heightened Latin American fears of the "Yankee menace."

Investments and intervention.

In the years that followed, United States investments in Latin America soared. North Americans bought sugar cane plantations in Cuba and copper mines in Chile. They built railroads and factories in Brazil and Argentina. In Mexico and Venezuela, they invested in oil wells. These investments benefited the wealthy; but not the majority of people in Latin America.

Financial interests led the United States to intervene in Latin America. In the early 1900s, the Dominican Republic was unable to pay its debts to American banks. The United States occupied the island, took over collection of its customs duties, and repaid the loans. United States marines remained in the Dominican Republic until 1924.

American forces also occupied Nicaragua and Haiti, and intervened in the affairs of Honduras six times. In each case, they stepped in to protect American lives and property or to support a government that favored American interests. [...]

Changing directions.

The growth of anti-American feelings and the beginning of the Great Depression led the United States to seek better relations with Latin America. In 1933, President Franklin D. Roosevelt announced the Good Neighbor Policy. He withdrew American marines from Haiti and agreed that “no state has the right to intervene in the internal or external affairs of another state.”

The United States, however, remained the dominant economic power in the region. American companies owned huge tracts of land, commercial farms, mines, and other valuable resources there. The United States was also the chief trading partner of most Latin American nations. [...]

Recent Trends

In recent years, the United States has encouraged the move toward democracy in Latin America. Although it continued to aid anticommunist forces, it also pressed rightist governments to make reforms.

El Salvador.

During the 1970s and 1980s, the United States gave massive military aid to El Salvador to help its government battle leftist guerrillas there. At the same time, it pressured the government to introduce land reform and hold free elections. Years of terror and turmoil had taken an enormous toll on the tiny country. In the early 1990s, the United Nations helped the rebels and government forces in El Salvador to negotiate a peace agreement.

Nicaragua.

[...] leftist Sandinistas gained power in Nicaragua after the overthrow of Anastasio Somoza. Fearing that Nicaragua would become another Cuba, the United States aided the contras in their guerrilla war against the Sandinista government. [...] The United States also imposed a trade embargo that crippled the Nicaraguan economy. The United States lifted the embargo and restored aid after Nicaragua held free elections and the Sandinistas lost.

The shadow of a giant.

As the Cold War ended, the fear of Soviet influence faded. Other issues, such as foreign debt and the illegal drug trade, became important in relations within the hemisphere.

Today, as in the past, Latin Americans have mixed feelings about the United States. They admire the rich material culture of their northern neighbor. At the same time, they resent its economic domination of the Western Hemisphere. [...]

Ahmad, Iftikar, Brodsky, Herbert; Crofts, Marylee Susan; Ellis, Elisabeth Gaynor: World Cultures. A Global Mosaic. New Jersey 2001, S. 505–509.

M2 Holding His End Up (by Fred Morgan):
John Bull: "It's really most extraordinary what training will do. Why, only the other day I trought that man unable to support himself." *Philadelphia Inquirer*, rpt. *The War of 1898 with Spain in Cartoons* (Chicago: Belford, Middlebrook & Co., 1898).

M3 Valuable Addition to the Repast
by Charles L. Bartholomew): Jamaica Ginger – "Uncle Sam, I thought you would be likely to want me after absorbing all that green fruit" *Minneapolis Journal* (Aug. 24, 1898), rpt. *The War of 1898 with Spain in Cartoons* (Chicago: Belford, Middlebrook & Co. 1898).

M4 Advice from One Who Knows
John Bull (to King Leopold): "Listen to me; I speak from experience. You can not colonize a country properly except by morality. I repeat it, by *morality*!" *Amsterdammer*, rpt. *Literary* Digest 34 (Jan. 5, 1907).

3.7 Post Colonization

M1 Defense of Imperialism in the Popular Press, 1962

At the time of decolonization many critics discussed publicly in the popular press the many misdeeds done by the imperialist countries. In contrast the British Francis Vivian Drake (1895–1971), former member of the Royal Flying corps and roving editor for the Reader's Digest, voiced a 'defense' of imperialism in his article "Don't Decry Colonialism" (1960), which was originally published in the Reader's Digest but was quickly translated and published throughout the world:

One of the most thrilling dramas of human history is unfolding under our eyes in Africa today. We are witnessing a continent more than three times the size of the United States, a vast storehouse of resources and manpower, plunging into self-rule, unready and explosive, while native politicians inflame men of unbelievable ignorance and Communist agents wait hopefully to take over from the politicians. The truth about this great drama, in which millions of black men are trying to claw their way up into civilization, has been obscured by a barrage of propaganda alleging that Western "colonialism" is resisting freedom and supporting enslavement. When compared with the facts these allegations turn out to be nonsense.

Colonialism is today a dead duck throughout the world, except in Moscow and Peiping. In Africa, 130,000,000 black men are now free citizens of the Belgian Congo, Camerons Republic, Dahomey, French Equatorial Africa, Ghana, Guinea, Kenya, Madagascar, Mali, Niger, Nigeria, Somalia and British Somaliland, Sudan, Tanganyika, Togoland and Volta, all of which have gained self-rule in the past four years or are in the final stages of achieving it. In countries like Rhodesia and Nyasaland the issue is still unsolved. But only in the Union of South Africa is a vicious type of colonialism still in existence, inflicted by a Nazi-type government which is trying to keep 9,600,000 black men in bondage. For the rest of Black Africa, the only enslavement left is to age-old tribal fetishes, witch doctors and primitive ignorance.

Still, Communist mouthings about colonialism not only have poisoned public opinion in neutral nations but have affected some Americans, who think of the word in connection with the American Revolution against British rule. They seem to forget that the men who wrote our Declaration were among the most idealistic, educated and politically enlightened men of their day, and that our new citizens had brought with them the best of the civilization of the Old World. In contrast, the vast majority of Africans today are uneducated and uncivilized. The struggle is to find enough of them, in any country, capable of self-government, and to educate enough of the voters to resist witch doctors and extremists.

If there is one place in Africa where the complexity of this problem is shown most vividly it is Kenya, the center of the Kenya-Uganda-Tanganyika group known as British East Africa. Here are the ingredients that trouble much of Africa: six million black men, divided into 33 tribes, educated only in their own tribal languages; the colonial power – in this case Britain – under tremendous pressure to get out; some 150,000 Asians, mostly from India, who run the stores and small businesses; and 60,000 white men who, with the Asians, have created a modern country out of a jungle, and now protest that they are about to be abandoned to ignorance and rapacity by the very government which induced them to settle the country in the first place.

The land itself, like so much of Africa, is startlingly beautiful. A visitor from America lands in Nairobi, only 16 flying hours from New York, often expecting to find a frontier town complete with feathered warriors, White Hunters, and lions behind every bush. Instead, he sees a beautiful modern city of nearly a quarter of a million, with gleaming white skyscrapers, wide streets, traffic lights, excellent hotels, stores and hospitals, with residential suburbs similar to those in California. The year-round climate is like an American summer.

A rail journey is a delight: a spotless train, sleeping compartments equal to our best, good food, and from the windows a view of fields of coffee, tea, pyrethrum, sisal, corn, being cultivated under justice and peace. One cannot help realizing that this is what British colonialism has brought to a country that without it would still be a primitive wilderness, for the land was not always rich and peaceful.

The first missionaries reported to Queen Victoria that it was a sink–hole of slave trading, tribal war and disease. The British ejected the Arab slavers, stopped the wars, attacked smallpox and sleeping sickness, and induced white men to settle the country. This proved to be a tough task. In the fierce bush of Africa nothing weak survives, be it man or beast. The soil is frequently inhospitable, crop failures were constant; but by hard work and sacrifice the colonials created modern Kenya, with a gross national product touching $500,000,000 a year.

Into this promising scene is now projected an outcry for Uhuru – absolute independence. The demand is completely valid. No one disputes it. The white man and Asians, however, do dispute the timing. The British government is putting into effect a new constitution under which Africans will have a majority in the Kenya legislature and head as many government departments as they have men competent to handle them. Three native ministers have already taken office. While the new government is learning its job, the British plan to retain the governor's veto power over financial improvidence, persecution of minorities and other excesses; but directly the new government demonstrates responsibility, the governor is to be withdrawn and Kenya will be on its own.

The African politicians violently oppose this moderate program. They demand independence now, immediately. Some of them threaten to pitch out all white men and Asians and seize their property. The place where these threats hit hardest and could cause the greatest injustice to white man and Africans alike is the White Highlands, north of Nairobi. This is the agricultural production center of Kenya. Its 13,000 square miles contain the best farms, well-kept and prosperous. They produce the bulk of Kenya's crops and most of the high-grade animals. They have been a white preserve, but are now to be thrown open by the British to African purchase.

To this proposal, a leading Luo tribe politician has replied that "it does nothing to redress the original injustice done to the African people when the Europeans took away their land." Not so. The Highlands, 50 years ago, were roamed by the fierce Masai, naked warriors armed with razor-sharp spears, living on blood tapped from the veins of their cattle. They prevented all farming and kept the Luo and other tribes hiding in the forests.

Of Kenya's 10,600,000 acres of arable land, only 20 per cent is farmed by white settlers-who, however, produce 80 per cent of the agricultural output of the country. In reverse, the Africans, with 80 per cent of the land, produce only 20 per cent. If all the white settlers were thrown out, the African farmers' average share of land would rise only from 15.5 acres to 16.8, and about 250,000 Africans now working on European land would be out of jobs. The agriculture-dependent industries of Kenya would collapse, unless the African farmers could quadruple their present rate of production per acre.

[...] The solution to the question of the treatment of minorities in Africa lies of course in education. The raw material is good. African children are smart. They have a passion to learn because it leads to good jobs; but there are not enough facilities. [...]

In the past, the record of colonial powers' pulling out too soon has not been a happy one. In India, the precipitate departure of the British cost three million lives in religious wars and other strife. In Ceylon, the economy is in chaos. In the Congo, just vacated in a hurry by the Belgians, ritual murder, tribal war and degeneration of government are all increasing. In the Sudan the excellent administrative services left by the British have been com-

promised. In Ghana, members of parliament who opposed the dictator, Dr. Nkrumah, were sentenced to prison and lashing.
Over this whole African scene the Communist radio maintains a ceaseless barrage of propaganda urging the natives to overthrow colonial influence. In Kenya itself local extremists, borrowing the patter, lead ignorant tribesmen into believing that Uhuru means deporting the Asians back to India and the whites back to Europe, taking over their businesses and farms and living the life of Riley. A farm laborer told his boss: "When Uhuru comes I am going to take your car and drive all over Kenya on whichever side of the road I please."
Self-rule is right. It is inevitable. But-as we see in the case of Kenya even the demand for civilized self-government could not have arisen but for the colonialism that brought the aspiration to a primitive people. Everyone would still be at the mercy of the tribesman with the longest spear. The greatest requirement in Africa is time – time to take over power in an orderly manner, to expand education and train administrators.
[...] It is through steps like these, by retaining the best of the old, that the new can be achieved. Workable self-rule will not come by parroting Communist slogans like "Western Imperialism," but by moderation and a sensible use of the legacy bequeathed to Black Africa by colonialism itself [...]

Snyder, Louis L. (Hrsg.): The Imperialism Reader. Documents and Readings on Modern Expansionism. Princeton (u.a.): D. van Nostrand Company New Jersey 1962, S. 136ff.

M2 Thomas Pakenham: Scramble for Africa

Thomas Pakenham (born 1933), an Anglo-Irish historian in the introduction to his prize-winning book 'The Scramble for Africa', 1991

The Scramble for Africa bewildered everyone, from the humblest African peasant to the master statesmen of the age, Lord Salisbury and Prince Bismarck.
Ever since Roman times, Europe had been nibbling at the mysterious continent to the south. By the mid-1870s, much was still mysterious. It was known that Africa straddled the equator with uncanny precision. But no explorer had penetrated far along the dangerous latitude of zero towards the interior. No one knew which was Africa's greatest river or where it led. Europeans pictured most of the continent as 'vacant': legally res nullius, a no-man's-land. If there were states and rulers, they were African. If there were treasures they were buried in African soil. But beyond the trading posts on the coastal fringe, and strategically important colonies in Algeria and South Africa, Europe saw no reason to intervene.
Suddenly, in half a generation, the Scramble gave Europe virtually the whole continent: including thirty new colonies and protectorates, 10 million square miles of new territory and 110 million dazed new subjects, acquired by one method or another. Africa was sliced up like a cake, the pieces swallowed by five rival nations – Germany, Italy, Portugal, France and Britain (with Spain taking some scraps) – and Britain and France were at each other's throats. At the centre, exploiting the rivalry, stood one enigmatic individual arid self-styled philanthropist, controlling the heart of the continent: Leopold II, King of the Belgians.
By the end of the century, the passions generated by the Scramble had helped to poison the political climate in Europe, brought Britain to the brink of a war with France, and precipitated a struggle with the Boers, the costliest, longest and bloodiest war since 1815 – and one of the most humiliating in British history . As for the pieces of the colonial cake, they have now become, ninety years later, for richer or for poorer (mainly for poorer) the forty-seven independent nations of Africa.
Why this undignified rush by the leaders of Europe to build empires in Africa? Anglo-French rivalry explains a great deal – but not enough. Historians are as puzzled now as the politicians were then. [...]
To these events historiography has added a pack of jostling theories. We have Eurocen-

tric explanations, like John Hobson's (and later Lenin's) theory that surplus capital in Europe was the driving force behind expansion into Africa; Afrocentric explanations where the emphasis is placed on sub-imperialisms in Africa itself; and combinations of the two [...] But there is no general explanation acceptable to historians – nor even agreement whether they should be expected to find one. [...]

In May 1873 David Livingstone, the celebrated missionary-explorer, died at Llala, in the unknown heart of the continent, and his sun-dried body was brought home to be buried in Westminster Abbey. From his brass-plated tomb under the nave, Livingstone sounded a call for a worldwide crusade to open up Africa. A new slave trade, organized by Swahili and Arabs in East Africa, was eating out the heart of the continent. Livingstone's answer was the '3 Cs': Commerce, Christianity and Civilization, a triple alliance of Mammon, God and social progress. Trade, not the gun, would liberate Africa.

The freelance promoters of the partition [...] are now half-forgotten. In their day they were famous – and infamous – feted as heroes, denounced as brutes or humbugs.

Each responded to Livingstone's call in his own fashion. But they all conceived of the crusade in terms of romantic nationalism. There were journalist-explorers like Henry Stanley, sailor-explorers like Pierre de Brazza, soldier-explorers like Frederick Lugard, pedagogue-explorers like Carl Peters, gold-arid-diamond tycoons like Cecil Rhodes. Most of them were outsiders of one kind or another but no less ardent nationalists for that. To imperialism – a kind of 'race patriotism' – they brought a missionary zeal. Not only would they save Africa from itself. Africa would be the saving of their own countries.

At first European governments were reluctant to intervene. But to most people in their electorates, there seemed a real chance of missing something. Africa was a lottery and a winning ticket might earn glittering prizes.

There were dreams of El Dorado, of diamond mines and goldfields criss-crossing the Sahara. In Europe these were the drab years of the Great Depression and mounting stocks of unsold Manchester cotton, Lyons silk and Hamburg gin. Perhaps Africa was the answer to the merchants' prayers. There might be new markets out there in this African garden of Eden, and tropical groves where the golden fruit could be plucked by willing brown hands.

Or perhaps the lottery would pay best in terms of prestige. Overseas empire would soothe the amour-propre of the French army, humiliated by its collapse in the Franco-Prussian war. And it would no less bolster the pride of the political parvenus of Europe, Germany's Second Reich and a newly united Italy. Then there were the diplomatic advantages. Cards drawn in the jungle could be played out in the chancelleries of Europe. No harm for Bismarck to consolidate his own position by making mischief between France and Britain. And what about a place in the sun for emigrants – and a way to retain as citizens all those young sons of the Reich now taking the boat and vanishing without trace in America? Give it a whirl, the 'colonial whirl' (*Kolonialtaumel*), in Bismarck's sardonic phrase.

In Britain, the Scramble was taken calmly – at first. Then there was growing resentment towards the intruders. Britain had pioneered the exploration and evangelization of Central Africa, and she felt a proprietary right to most of the continent. Besides, there was a vital interest at stake for Britain. As the only great maritime Empire, she needed to prevent her rivals obstructing the steamer routes to the East, via Suez and the Cape. That meant digging in at both ends of Africa.

[...] That was not the way Africans perceived the Scramble. There was a fourth 'c' – conquest – and it gradually predominated. At first European expeditions were too weak to challenge African rulers. It was safer to use blank treaty forms, explained away by an empire-minded missionary, than to use live ammunition.

But paper imperialism soon proved inadequate. When effective occupation became necessary to establish a good title, conflict became inevitable. The African rulers best equipped to resist were understandably those who depended on violence themselves: African imperialists like King Cetshwayo of the Zulu, King Lobengula of the Ndebele, the Emperor Menelik of Abyssinia, the Mahdi in the Sudan, and Africa's twin white tribes, the Boers of the Transvaal and Boers of the Orange Free State.

Soon the Maxim gun – not trade or the cross – became the symbol of the age in Africa [...]. Most of the battles were cruelly one-sided [...]. At Omdurman, British officers counted 10,000 Sudanese dead or dying in the sand. They made no effort to help the 15,000 wounded.

Atrocities were commonplace during the first phase of occupation by the Powers. When German brutality in South West Africa provoked a revolt by the Hereros, the German general, Lothar von Trotha, issued a *Vernichtungbefehl* ('extermination order') against the whole tribe, women and children included. About 20,000 of them were driven away from the wells to die in the Omaheke desert.

Europe had imposed its will on Africa at the point of a gun. It was a lesson that would be remembered, fifty years later, when Africa came to win its independence. [...]

Pakenham, Thomas: The Scramble for Africa. 1876–1912. London: Weidenfeld and Nicolson 1991, S. XV–XIX.

M3 Epilogue

Bonnie G. Smith, professor of History at Rutgers University (New Jersey's State University) writes an 'epilogue' to imperialism in her collection of source materials "Imperialism: A History in Documents", 2000

All the imperialist nations claimed to be benefiting those they conquered and oppressed. In this regard Japan was no different from the United States justifying its conquest of the Philippines or the great European powers plundering the African and Asian continents. The difference is that the Japanese expansion of the 1930s and early 1940s proved to be the final blow to the age of high imperialism that had begun in the 19th century. Where it did not destroy the European grasp, Japanese conquest weakened it. It contributed to the general catastrophe of World War II that spread so much disorder globally. When the war ended, empires collapsed.

Despite its disintegration after World War II, imperialism as a system of direct political rule of conquered areas left an enduring legacy. It had truly internationalized commerce and politics because of the systems of rapid transportation and communication embodied in the railroad, steamship, telegraph, and telephone involved in imperialism's triumph. In these circumstances Western culture lost the distinctiveness that it might have retained from Europe's relative isolation. Instead, Western civilization became a culture profoundly dependent on taking and incorporating ideas, customs, and resources from the rest of the world. Although there was a great deal of borrowing in the other direction as well, some have argued that imperialism had far less effect outside the West in cultural terms. Instead, the real effect of imperialism elsewhere was in its plunder and rapacious devastation of resources, whether that plundering was committed by the English, Belgians, Russians, Americans, or Japanese. [...]

Another legacy of imperialism is the incredible and increasing global violence that has since the 19th century killed hundreds of millions in colonial conquest and forced labor, world wars, wars of liberation, and civil wars – all of them connected in one way or another to imperialism and its aftermath. It is one of imperialism's many paradoxes that while it made people more aware than ever before of the world's multiple races, accomplishments, and cultures, it set a trend of pitting humans against one another in an orgy of conquest, competition, and hatred. Yet at the same time, around the globe population soared, health improved, technology became more modern, and concern for human rights advanced.

A final legacy and paradox of imperialism is that its end saw the world increasingly divided between prosperous peoples of the former imperial powers and poorer peoples who had once been colonized. Differences in wealth became greater, and a new or neo-imperialism had replaced the old. This neo-imperialism was based – as it had been before political conquest in the 19th century – on trading superiority and on a culture of curiosity, acquisitiveness, and conquest. Although the age of high imperialism ended long ago, it continues to shape our present world.

Smith, Bonnie G.: Imperialism. A History in Documents. Oxford 2000, S. 164–165.

M4 Additional: Food for Thought

A somewhat radical and a little one-sided, neo-Marxist but stirring and thought provoking essay by the well-known African intellectual Amir Samin on the contemporary phenomenon globalization as the third phase of imperialism can be found here:

http://skeptically.org/polrec/id6.html

4. Germany in Perspective

4.1 The Outbreak of World War I in Perspective

The war in 1914 came as no surprise. For more than a decade a sense of crisis had loomed large over Europe and there had been many occasions which might have triggered an earlier beginning of the war. The rapid changes countries had had to come to terms with due to the Industrial Revolution and the effects of imperialism had led to numerous conflicts.
In the age of nationalism the Balkans with its many nationalities but without a nation state had long been one of the most virulent trouble spots in Europe. It was the shot fired in Sarajevo that proved to be the incident that could no longer be dealt with by diplomatic means and which finally sparked off the Great War as it is called in Great Britain. From the following reports we get an idea as to the mood of the public in Vienna, Paris and London. The perspective of the political leaders can then be traced from speech extracts by Prime Minister Asquith and President Wilson; the dissenting view of American liberals can be seen from the remarks of a leading American intellectual of the day who represents the line of thought of American Progressivism to which Woodrow Wilson belonged as well. The ideas behind the German public mood are given to us by Friedrich von Bernhardi.

4.1.1 The Outbreak of War in Three European Capitals

It is very difficult to assess public opinion concerning pre-opinion poll days. Not all social groups had access to media that would leave traces of their sentiments for historians to find. In case of war there is the additional problem of censorship or, at least, of strong government influence on published opinion. When the bestselling Daily Mirror reports on the declaration of war in its 4 August 1914 edition it says on the front page: "Huge Crowds Cheer Their Majesties at Palace". This may be true for the public reaction in London but whether it is also true for the rural counties we cannot tell.
The following selections show public reactions to the outbreak of war in three European capitals seen through the eyes of intellectuals.

M1 VIENNA: The Rushing Feeling of Fraternity

Stefan Zweig (1881 – 1942), Austrian author, volunteered in WW I but then became a pacifist. As an emigrant he and his wife committed suicide in Brazil in 1942.

The next morning I was in Austria. In every station placards had been put up announcing general mobilization. The trains were filled with fresh recruits, banners were flying, music sounded, and in Vienna I found the entire city in a tumult. The first shock at the news of war – the war that no one, people or government, had wanted – the war which had slipped, much against their will, out of the clumsy hands of the diplomats who had been bluffing and toying with it, had suddenly been transformed into enthusiasm. There were parades in the streets, flags, ribbons, and music burst forth everywhere, young recruits were marching triumphantly, their faces lighting up at the cheering – they, the John Does and Richard Roes who usually go unnoticed and uncelebrated.
And to be truthful, I must acknowledge that there was a majestic, rapturous, and even seductive something in this first outbreak of the people from which one could escape only

with difficulty. And in spite of all my hatred and aversion for war I should not like to have missed the memory of those first days. As never before, thousands and hundreds of thousands felt what they should have felt in peace time, that they belonged together. A city of two million, a country of nearly fifty million, in that hour felt that they were participating in world history, in a moment which would never recur, and that each one was called upon to cast his infinitesimal self into the glowing mass, there to be purified of all selfishness. All differences of class, rank, and language were flooded over at that moment by the rushing feeling of fraternity. Strangers spoke to one another in the streets, people who had avoided each other for years shook hands, everywhere one saw excited faces. Each individual experienced an exaltation of his ego, he was no longer the isolated person of former times, he had been incorporated into the mass, he was part of the people, and his person, his hitherto unnoticed person, had been given meaning. [...] Even mothers with their grief, and women with their fears, were ashamed to manifest their quite natural emotions in the face of this first transformation. But it is quite possible that a deeper, more secret power was at work in this frenzy. So deeply, so quickly did the tide break over humanity that, foaming over the surface, it churned up the depths, the subconscious primitive instincts of the human animal – that which Freud so meaningfully calls "the revulsion from culture," the desire to break out of the conventional bourgeois world of codes and statutes, and to permit the primitive instincts of the blood to rage at will. [...] [W]hat did the great mass know of war in 1914, after nearly half a century of peace? They did not know war, they had hardly given it a thought. It had become legendary, and distance had made it seem romantic and heroic. [...] "We'll be home at Christmas," the recruits shouted laughingly to their mothers in August of 1914. [...] A rapid excursion into the romantic, a wild, manly adventure – that is how the war of 1914 was painted in the imagination of the simple man, and the young people were honestly afraid that they might miss this most wonderful and exciting experience of their lives; that is why they hurried to the colors, and that is why they shouted and sang in the trains that carried them to the slaughter; wildly and feverishly the red wave of blood coursed through the veins of the entire nation."

Stefan Zweig: The World of Yesterday, 1941, pp.223–226, (autobiography).

M2 PARIS: That Fabulous Day

In "After Fifty Years," Roland Doregeles (1886–1973), a distinguished French writer, recalls the mood in Paris at the outbreak of the war.

"It's come! It's posted at the district mayor's office," a passerby shouted to me as he ran. I reached the Rue Drouot in one leap and shouldered through the mob that had already filled the courtyard to approach the fascinating white sheet pasted to the door. I read the message at a glance, then reread it slowly, word for word, to convince myself that it was true:

THE FIRST DAY OF MOBILIZATION WILL BESUNDAY, AUGUST 2

Only three lines, written hastily by a hand that trembled. It was an announcement to a million and a half Frenchmen.

The people who had read it moved away, stunned, while others crowded in, but this silent numbness did not last. Suddenly a heroic wind lifted their heads. What? War, was it? Well, then, let's go! Without any signal, the "Marseillaise" poured from thousands of throats, sheafs of flags appeared at windows, and howling processions rolled out on the boulevards. Each column brandished a placard: ALSACE VOLUNTEERS, JEWISH VOLUNTEERS, POLISH VOLUNTEERS. They hailed one another above the bravos of the crowd, and this human torrent, swelling at every corner, moved on to circle around the Place de la Concorde, before the statue of Strasbourg banked with flowers, then flowed toward the Place de la Republique, where mobs from Belleville and the Faubourg St.

Antoine yelled themselves hoarse on the refrain from the great days, "Aux armes, citoyens!" (To arms, citizens!) But this time it was better than a song.

To gather the news for my paper, I ran around the city in every direction. At the Cours la Reine I saw the fabled cuirassiers [cavalry] in their horsetail plumes march by, and at the Rue La Fayette footsoldiers in battle garb with women throwing flowers and kisses to them. In a marshaling yard I saw guns being loaded, their long, thin barrels twined around with branches and laurel leaves, while troops in red breeches piled gaily into delivery vans they were scrawling with challenges and caricatures. Young and old, civilians and military men burned with the same excitement. It was like Brotherhood Day.

Dead tired but still exhilarated, I got back to L'Homme Libre and burst into the office of Georges Clemenceau*, our chief.

"What is Paris saying?" he asked me. "It's singing, sir!" "Then everything will be all right. ..." His old patriot's heart was not wrong; no cloud marred that fabulous day. ...

Less than twenty-four hours later, seeing their old dreams of peace crumble [socialist workers] would stream out into the boulevards . ... [but] they would break into the "Marseillaise," not the "Internationale"; they would cry, "To Berlin!," not "Down with war!"

What did they have to defend, these black nailed patriots? Not even a shack, an acre to till, indeed hardly a patch of ground reserved at the Pantin Cemetery; yet they would depart, like their rivals of yesterday, a heroic song on their lips and a flower in their guns. No more poor or rich, proletariats or bourgeois, right-wingers or militant leftists; there were only Frenchmen.

Beginning the next day, thousands of men eager to fight would jostle one another outside recruiting offices, waiting to join up. Men who could have stayed home, with their wives and children or an imploring mama. But no. The word "duty" had meaning for them, and the word "country" had regained its splendor.

I close my eyes, and they appear to me, those volunteers on the great day; then I see them again in the old kepi [military cap] or blue helmet, shouting, "Here!" when somebody called for men for a raid, or hurling themselves into an attack with fixed bayonets, and I wonder, and I question their bloody [ghosts].

Tell me, comrades in eternal silence, would you have besieged the enlistment offices with the same enthusiasm, would you have fought such a courageous fight had you known that fifty years later those men in gray knit caps or steel helmets you were ordered to kill would no longer be enemies and that we would have to open our arms to them? Wouldn't the heroic "Let's go!" you shouted as you cleared the parapets have stuck in your throats? Deep in the grave where you dwell, don't you regret your sacrifice? "Why did we fight? Why did we let ourselves get killed" This is the murmur of a million and a half voices rising from the bowels of the earth, and we, the survivors, do not know what to answer.

(Translated from the French by Sally Abeles)

http://teachers.sduhsd.k12.ca.us/tpsocialsciences/world_history/world_war1/celebration.htm

* Georges Clemenceau (1841–1929), editor, French Prime Minister 1906–1909, 1917–1920

M3 LONDON: The Steep Slope to Primitive Barbarism

Bertrand Russell (1872–1950), British mathematician, philosopher, Nobel Laureate and peace activist, was imprisoned for being a pacifist during WW I

A month ago Europe was a peaceful group of nations: if an Englishman killed a German, he was hanged. Now, if an Englishman kills a German, or if a German kills an Englishman, he is a patriot. We scan the newspapers with greedy eyes for news of slaughter, and rejoice when we read of innocent young men, blindly obedient to the world of command, mown down in thousands by the machine-gun of Liege. [...]

Those who saw the London crowds, during the nights leading up to the Declaration of War saw a whole population , hitherto peaceable and humane, precipitated in a few days down the steep slope to primitive barbarism, letting loose, in a moment, the instincts of hatred and blood lust against which the whole fabric of society has been raised. "Patriots" in all countries acclaim this brutal orgy as a noble determination to vindicate the right; reason and mercy are swept away in one great flood of hatred; dim abstractions of unimaginable wickedness – Germany to us and the French, Russia to the Germans – conceal the simple fact that the enemy are men, like ourselves, neither better nor worse – men who love their homes and the sunshine, and all the simple pleasures of common lives. [...]

The friends of progress have been betrayed by their chosen leaders, who have plunged the country suddenly into a war which must cause untold misery, and which an overwhelming majority of those who voted for the present Government believe to be as unwise as it is wicked. No man whose liberalism is genuine can herea after support the members of the present Cabinet.

Bertrand Russell, from a letter published by the Nation, on 15 August 1914, taken from: Perry, M. et al. (ed.): Sources of the Western Tradition, 5th ed., Houghton Mifflin, Boston 2003, p. 306 and from http://www.spartacus.schoolnet.co.uk/TUrussell.htm (parts 1+3)

4.1.2 German, British and American Perspectives

M1 British Prime Minister Asquith's Address to Parliament, 6 August 1914

Herbert H. Asquith (1852–1928), Liberal Prime Minister, 1908–1916

With the utmost reluctance and with infinite regret, His Majesty's Government have been compelled to put this country in a state of war with what for many years and indeed generations past has been a friendly Power. [...]

I am entitled to say, and I do so on behalf of this country – I speak not for a party, I speak for the country as a whole – that we made every effort any Government could possibly make for peace.

But this war has been forced upon us. What is it we are fighting for? Every one knows, and no one knows better than the Government, the terrible, incalculable suffering, economic, social, personal and political, which war, and especially a war between the Great Powers of the world, must entail. [...]

If I am asked what we are fighting for I reply in two sentences: In the first place, to fulfil a solemn international obligation, an obligation which, if it had been entered into between private persons in the ordinary concerns of life, would have been regarded as an obligation not only of law but of honour, which no self-respecting man could possibly have repudiated.

I say, secondly, we are fighting to vindicate the principle which, in these days when force, material force, sometimes seems to be the dominant influence and factor in the development of mankind, we are fighting to vindicate the principle that small nationalities are not to be crushed, in defiance of international good faith, by the arbitrary will of a strong and overmastering Power.

I do not believe any nation ever entered into a great controversy – and this is one of the greatest history will ever know – with a clearer conscience and a stronger conviction that it is fighting, not for aggression, not for the maintenance even of its own selfish interest, but that it is fighting in defence of principles the maintenance of which is vital to the civilization of the world.

With a full conviction, not only of the wisdom and justice, but of the obligations which lay upon us to challenge this great issue, we are entering into the struggle. Let us now make sure that all the resources, not only of this United Kingdom, but of the vast Empire of which it is the centre, shall be thrown into the scale.

Source: Source Records of the Great War, Vol. I, ed. Charles F. Horne, National Alumni 1923, taken from: www.firstworldwar.com/source/asquithspeechtoparliament.htm

M2 President Wilson's Declaration of Neutrality, 19 August, 1914

Woodrow Wilson (1856–1924), President of Princeton University, U.S. President 1913–1921

[...] our duty as the one great nation at peace, the one people holding itself ready to play a part of impartial mediation and speak the counsels of peace and accommodation, not as a partisan, but as a friend.

I venture, therefore, my fellow countrymen, to speak a solemn word of warning to you against that deepest, most subtle, most essential breach of neutrality which may spring out of partisanship, out of passionately taking sides. The United States must be neutral in fact, as well as in name, during these days that are to try men's souls. We must be impartial in thought, as well as action, must put a curb upon our sentiments, as well as upon every transaction that might be construed as a preference of one party to the struggle before another.

Woodrow Wilson, Message to Congress, 63rd Cong., 2d Sess., Senate Doc. No. 566 (Washington, 1914), pp. 3–4.

M3 19 January, 1917: The Zimmermann Note to the German Minister to Mexico

Secret telegram sent from the Foreign Office in Berlin to the German ambassador in Mexico; the text was decoded by the British. Arthur Zimmermann (1864–1940) was 'Staatssekretär' in the German Foreign Office, 11/1916–8/1917, but the literal translation 'German Foreign Secretary' has led to the misunderstanding in the English speaking world even today that he was the German Foreign Minister. Zimmermann had to step down from office when he acknowledged the authenticity of the telegram.

To the German Minister to Mexico

Berlin, January 19, 1917

On the first of February we intend to begin submarine warfare unrestricted. In spite of this, it is our intention to endeavour to keep neutral the United States of America.

If this attempt is not successful, we propose an alliance on the following basis with Mexico: That we shall make war together and together make peace. We shall give general financial support, and it is understood that Mexico is to reconquer the lost territory in New Mexico, Texas, and Arizona. The details are left to you for settlement [...]

You are instructed to inform the President of Mexico of the above in the greatest confidence as soon as it is certain that there will be an outbreak of war with the United States and suggest that the President of Mexico, on his own initiative, should communicate with Japan suggesting adherence at once to this plan; at the same time, offer to mediate between Germany and Japan.

Please call to the attention of the President of Mexico that the employment of ruthless submarine warfare now promises to compel England to make peace in a few months.

Zimmermann
(Secretary of State)

Source: Source Records of the Great War, Vol. V, ed. Charles F. Horne, National Alumni 1923; taken from: http://www.firstworldwar.com/source/zimmermann.htm

M4 Woodrow Wilson's War Message to Congress, April 2, 1917

Woodrow Wilson (1856–1924), President of Princeton University, U.S. President 1913–1921

Our object is to vindicate the principles of peace and justice in the life of the world as against selfish and autocratic power and to set up among the really free and self-governed peoples of the world such a concert of purpose and of action as will henceforth ensure the observance of those principles. Neutrality is no longer feasible or desirable where the peace of the world is involved and the freedom of its peoples, and the menace to that peace and freedom lies in the existence of autocratic governments backed by organized force which is controlled wholly by their will, not by the will of their people. We have seen the last of neutrality in such circumstances. We are at the beginning of an age in which it will be insisted that the same standards of conduct and of responsibility for wrong done shall be observed among nations and their governments that are observed among the individual citizens of civilized states.

We have no quarrel with the German people. We have no feeling toward them but one of sympathy and friendship. It was not upon their impulse that their government acted in entering this war. It was not with their previous knowledge or approval. It was a war determined upon as wars used to be determined upon in the old, unhappy days when peoples were nowhere consulted by their rulers and wars were provoked and waged in the interest of dynasties or of little groups of ambitious men who were accustomed to use their fellowmen as pawns and tools.

Self-governed nations do not fill their neighbor states with spies or set the course of intrigue to bring about some critical posture of affairs which will give them an opportunity to strike and make conquest. Such designs can be successfully worked out only under cover and where no one has the right to ask questions. Cunningly contrived plans of deception or aggression, carried, it may be, from generation to generation, can be worked out and kept from the light only within the privacy of courts or behind the carefully guarded confidences of a narrow and privileged class. They are happily impossible where public opinion commands and insists upon full information concerning all the nation's affairs. [...]

One of the things that has served to convince us that the Prussian autocracy was not and could never be our friend is that from the very outset of the present war it has filled our unsuspecting communities and even our offices of government with spies and set criminal intrigues everywhere afoot against our national unity of counsel, our peace within and without, our industries and our commerce. Indeed, it is now evident that its spies were here even before the war began; and it is unhappily not a matter of conjecture but a fact proved in our courts of justice that the intrigues which have more than once come perilously near to disturbing the peace and dislocating the industries of the country have been carried on at the instigation, with the support, and even under the personal direction of official agents of the Imperial government accredited to the government of the United States.

Even in checking these things and trying to extirpate them, we have sought to put the most generous interpretation possible upon them because we knew that their source lay, not in any hostile feeling or purpose of the German people toward us (who were no doubt as ignorant of them as we ourselves were) but only in the selfish designs of a government that did what it pleased and told its people nothing. But they have played their part in serving to convince us at last that that government entertains no real friendship for us and means to act against our peace and security at its convenience. That it means to stir up enemies against us at our very doors the intercepted note to the German minister at Mexico City is eloquent evidence.

We are accepting this challenge of hostile purpose because we know that in such a government, following such methods, we can never have a friend; and that in the presence of its organized power, always lying in wait to accomplish we know not what purpose, there can be no assured security for the democratic governments of the world. We are now about to accept gage of battle with this natural foe to liberty and shall, if necessary, spend the whole force of the nation to check and nullify its pretensions and its power. We are glad, now that we see the facts with no veil of false pretense about them, to fight thus for the ultimate peace of the world and for the liberation of its peoples, the German peoples included: for the rights of nations great and small and the privilege of men everywhere to choose their way of life and of obedience.

The world must be made safe for democracy. Its peace must be planted upon the tested foundations of political liberty. We have no selfish ends to serve. We desire no conquest, no dominion. We seek no indemnities for ourselves, no material compensation for the sacrifices we shall freely make. We are but one of the champions of the rights of mankind. We shall be satisfied when those rights have been made as secure as the faith and the freedom of nations can make them.

Just because we fight without rancor and without selfish object, seeking nothing for ourselves but what we shall wish to share with all free peoples, we shall, I feel confident, conduct our operations as belligerents without passion and ourselves observe with proud punctilio the principles of right and of fair play we profess to be fighting for.

Source: 65 Congress, I Session, Senate Document No. 5, taken from: http://www.mtholyoke.edu/acad/intrel/ww18.htm

M5 The War and the Intellectuals

Randolph Bourne (1886–1918), progressivist American intellectual. He kept a 'War Diary' in a magazine (The Seven Arts) and in this magazine he published the bitter article from which the following excerpt is taken.

To the American academic mind of 1914 defense of war was inconceivable. From Bernhardi it recoiled as from blasphemy, little dreaming that two years later would find it creating its own cleanly reasons for imposing military service on the country and for talking of the rough rude currents of health and regeneration that war would send through the American body politic. They would have thought anyone mad who talked of shipping American men by the hundreds of thousands – conscripts – to die on the fields of France. Such a spiritual change seems catastrophic when we shoot our minds back to those days when neutrality was a proud thing. But the intellectual progress has been so gradual that the country retains little sense of the irony. The war sentiment, begun so gradually but so perseveringly by the preparedness advocates who come from the ranks of big business, caught hold of one after another of the intellectual groups. With the aid of Roosevelt, the murmurs became a monotonous chant, and finally a chorus so mighty that to be out of it was at first to be disreputable and finally almost obscene. And slowly a strident rant was worked up against Germany which compared very creditably with the German fulminations against the greedy power of England. The nerve of the war-feeling centered, of course, in the richer and older clases of the Atlantic seaboard, and was keenest where there were French or English business and particularly social connections. The sentiment then spread over the country as a class-phenomenon, touching everywhere those upper-class elements in each section who identified themselves with this Eastern ruling group. It must never be forgotten that in every community it was the least liberal and least democratic elements among whom the preparedness and later the war sentiment was found. The farmers were apathetic, the small business men and workingmen are still apathetic towards the war. The election was a vote of confidence of these latter classes in a President who would keep the faith of neutrality. The intellectuals, in other words, have identified themselves with the least democratic forces in American life. [...]

We go to war to save the world from subjugation! But the German intellectuals went to war to save their culture from barbarization! And the French went to war to save their beautiful France! And the English to save international honor! And Russia, most altruistic and self-sacrificing of all, to save a small State from destruction. Whence is our miraculous intuition of our moral spotlessness? Whence our confidence that history will not unravel huge economic and imperialist forces upon which our rationalizations float like bubbles?

Randolph Bourne, "The War and the Intellectuals," Seven Arts 2,1917, pp. 133–136.

M6 The Next War

Friedrich von Bernhardi, (1849–1930), German general, chief historian to the German General Staff (1898–1901) and bestselling author with his 1911 book 'Germany and the Next War' from which the following excerpt is taken.

We have fought in the last great wars for our national union and our position among the Powers of *Europe*; we now must decide whether we wish to develop into and maintain a *World Empire*, and procure for German spirit and German ideas that fit recognition which has been hitherto withheld from them.

Have we the energy to aspire to that great goal? Are we prepared to make the sacrifices which such an effort will doubtless cost us? or are we willing to recoil before the hostile forces, and sink step by step lower in our economic, political, and national importance? That is what is involved in our decision.
"To be, or not to be," is the question which is put to us today (...).
We must make it quite clear to ourselves that there can be no standing still, no being satisfied for us, but only progress or retrogression, and that it is tantamount to retrogression when we are contented with our present place among the nations of Europe, while all our rivals are straining with desperate energy, even at the cost of our rights, to extend their power. The process of our decay would set in gradually and advance slowly so long as the struggle against us was waged with peaceful weapons; the living generation would, perhaps, be able to continue to exist in peace and comfort. But should a war be forced upon us by stronger enemies under conditions unfavorable to us, then, if our arms met with disaster, our political downfall would not be delayed, and we should rapidly sink down. The future of German nationality would be sacrificed, an independent German civilization would not long exist, and the blessings for which German blood has flowed in streams spiritual and moral liberty, and the profound and lofty aspirations of German thought would for long ages be lost to mankind.
If, as is right, we do not wish to assume the responsibility for such a catastrophe, we must have the courage to strive with every means to attain that increase of power which we are entitled to claim, even at the risk of a war with numerically superior foes. (...)
We must rouse in our people the unanimous wish for power in this sense, together with the determination to sacrifice on the altar of patriotism, no only life and property, but also private views and preferences in the interests of the common welfare. Then alone shall we discharge our great duties of the future, grow into a World Power, and stamp a great part of humanity with the impress of the German spirit. If, on the contrary, we persist in that dissipation of energy which now marks our political life, there is imminent fear that in the great contest of the nations, which we must inevitably face, we shall be dishonorably beaten; that days of disaster await us in the future, and that once again, as in the days of our former degradation, the poet's lament will be heard:
"O Germany, thy oaks still stand
But thou art fallen, glorious land!" [Koerner]

Friedrich von Bernhardi, Germany and the Next War (New York, 1914) [Translated by Allen H. Powles.] http://h-net.org/~german/gtext/kaiserreich/bernhardi.html

M7 1914: Manifesto of the Ninety-Three German Intellectuals to the Civilized World

As representatives of German Science and Art, we hereby protest to the civilized world against the lies and calumnies with which our enemies are endeavoring to stain the honor of Germany in her hard struggle for existence in a struggle that has been forced on her.
The iron mouth of events has proved the untruth of the fictitious German defeats; consequently misrepresentation and calumny are all the more eagerly at work. As heralds of truth we raise our voices against these.
It is not true that Germany is guilty of having caused this war. Neither the people, the Government, nor the "Kaiser" wanted war [...].
It is not true that we trespassed in neutral Belgium. It has been proved that France and England had resolved on such a trespass, and it has likewise been proved that Belgium had agreed to their doing so. It would have been suicide on our part not to have been beforehand.
It is not true that the life and property of a single Belgian citizen was injured by our soldiers without the bitterest defense having made it necessary [...]
It is not true that our troops treated Louvain brutally. Furious inhabitants having treacherously fallen upon them in their quarters, our

troops with aching hearts were obliged to fire a part of the town, as punishment. The greatest part of Louvain has been preserved [...]. *It is not true* that our warfare pays no respects to international laws. It knows no undisciplined cruelty. But in the east, the earth is saturated with the blood of women and children unmercifully butchered by the wild Russian troops, and in the west, dumdum bullets mutilate the breasts of our soldiers. [...]
It is not true that the combat against our so-called militarism is not a combat against our civilization, as our enemies hypocritically pretend it is. Were it not for German militarism, German civilization would long since have been extirpated. [...]
We cannot wrest the poisonous weapon -- the lie -- out of the hands of our enemies. All we can do is proclaim to all the world, that our enemies are giving false witness against us ...
Have faith in us! Believe, that we shall carry on this war to the end as a civilized nation, to whom the legacy of a Goethe, a Beethoven, and a Kant, is just as sacred as its own hearths and homes.
EMIL VON BEHRING, Professor of Medicine, Marburg
Prof. PAUL EHRLICH, Frankfurt on the Main
FRITZ HABER, Professor of Chemistry, Berlin
ERNST HAECKL, Professor of Zoology, Jena
Prof. ADOLF VON HARNACK, General Director of the Royal Library, Berlin
KARL LAMPRECHT, Professor of History, Leipzig
MAX LIEBERMANN, Berlin
MAX PLANCK, Professor of Physics, Berlin
Prof. MAX REINHARDT, Director of the German Theatre, Berlin
WILHELM ROENTGEN, Professor of Physics, Munich
GUSTAV VON SCHMOLLER, Professor of National Economy, Berlin [...]
http://net.lib.byu.edu/~rdh7/wwi/1914/93intell.html

4.1.3 War Aims

WW I represented a new kind of war, with a new kind of warfare, based on new weapons. It could be anticipated that this war would cost an unprecedented number of lives – in the end about 10 million soldiers did not return home.
To get involved in such a war demanded as a rationale, compelling reasons and motivations. We will take a look at German, British and American war aims as expressed by the leading politicians of these countries. We should take special note of U.S. President Wilson's 14 points because they opened up a long-term perspective and because they represented a break with the traditionally isolationist U.S. foreign policy.

M1 Germany's War Aims September, 1914
Theobald von Bethmann-Hollweg (1856–1921), German Chancellor, 1909–1917

The general aim of the war is security for the German Reich in west and east for all imaginable time. For this purpose France must be so weakened as to make her revival as a great power impossible for all time. Russia must be thrust back as far as possible from Germany's eastern frontier and her domination over the non-Russian vassal peoples broken.
1. France. The military to decide whether we should demand cession of Belfort and western slopes of the Vosges, razing of fortresses and cession of coastal strip from Dunkirk to Boulogne.
The ore-field of Briey, which is necessary for the supply of ore for our industry, to be ceded in any case. Further, a war indemnity, to be

paid in instalments; it must be high enough to prevent France from spending any considerable sums on armaments in the next 15–20 years.

Furthermore: a commercial treaty which makes France economically dependent on Germany, secures the French market for our exports and makes it possible to exclude British commerce from France. This treaty must secure for us financial and industrial freedom of movement in France in such fashion that German enterprises can no longer receive different treatment from French.

2. *Belgium.* Liége and Verviers to be attached to Prussia, a frontier strip of the province of Luxemburg to Luxemburg.

Question whether Antwerp, with a corridor to Liége, should also be annexed remains open.

At any rate Belgium, even if allowed to continue to exist as a state, must be reduced to a vassal state, must allow us to occupy any militarily important ports, must place her coast at our disposal in military respects, must become economically a German province. Given such a solution, which offers the advantages of annexation without its inescapable domestic political disadvantages, French Flanders with Dunkirk, Calais and Boulogne, where most of the population is Flemish, can without danger be attached to this unaltered Belgium. The competent quarters will have to judge the military value of this position against England.

3. *Luxemburg.* Will become a German federal state and will receive a strip of the present Belgian province of Luxemburg and perhaps the corner of Longwy.

4. We must create a central European economic association through common customs treaties, to include France, Belgium, Holland, Denmark, Austria-Hungary, Poland "sic", and perhaps Italy, Sweden and Norway. This association […] will be under German leadership and must stabilise Germany's economic dominance over Mitteleuropa.

5. *The question of colonial acquisitions,* where the first aim is the creation of a continuous Central African colonial empire, will be considered later, as will that of the aims to be realised vis-à-vis Russia.

From Fritz Fischer, *Germany's Aims in the First World War,* W. W. Norton & Company, Inc., 1967.

M2 Prime Minister Lloyd George on British War Aims, 5 January, 1918:

David Lloyd George (1863–1945), Liberal Prime Minister, 1916–1922

We may begin by clearing away some misunderstandings and stating what we are not fighting for. We are not fighting a war of aggression against the German people. Their leaders have persuaded them that they are fighting a war of self-defence against a league of rival nations bent on the destruction of Germany. That is not so. The destruction or disruption of Germany or the German people has never been a war aim with us from the first day of this war to this day. Most reluctantly, and indeed quite unprepared for the dreadful ordeal, we were forced to join in this war in self-defence. In defence of the violated public law of Europe, and in vindication of the most solemn treaty obligation on which the public system of Europe rested, and on which Germany had ruthlessly trampled in her invasion of Belgium, we had to join in the struggle or stand aside and see Europe go under and brute force triumph over public right and international justice. It was only the realization of that dreadful alternative that forced the British people into the war. […]

- Our point of view is that the adoption of a really democratic constitution by Germany would be the most convincing evidence that in her the old spirit of military domination had indeed died in this war, and would make it much easier for us to conclude a broad democratic peace with her. But, after all, that is a question for the German people to decide. […]
- [W]e feel that government with the consent of the governed must be the basis of any territorial settlement in this war. […]
- We believe, however, that an independent Poland comprising all those genuinely Polish elements who desire to form part of it, is an

urgent necessity for the stability of Western Europe. [...]

• With regard to the German colonies, I have repeatedly declared that they are held at the disposal of a conference whose decision must have primary regard to the wishes and interests of the native inhabitants of such colonies. None of those territories are inhabited by Europeans. [...]

• Finally, there must be reparation for injuries done in violation of international law.

[...] If, then, we are asked what we are fighting for, we reply as, we have often replied: we are fighting for a just and lasting peace, and we believe that be fore permanent peace can be hoped for three conditions must be fulfilled; firstly, the sanctity of treaties must be established; secondly, a territorial settlement must be secured, based on the right of self-determination or the consent of the governed, and, lastly, we must seek by the creation of some international organization to limit the burden of armaments and diminish the probability of war.

Authorized Version as published by the British Government, taken from: http://net.lib.byu.edu/~rdh7/wwi/1918/waraims.html

M3 President Woodrow Wilson's Fourteen Points, 8 January, 1918

We entered this war because violations of right had occurred which touched us to the quick and made the life of our own people impossible unless they were corrected and the world secure once for all against their recurrence. What we demand [...] is that the world be made fit and safe to live in; and particularly that it be made safe for every peace-loving nation which, like our own, wishes to live its own life, determine its own institutions, be assured of justice and fair dealing by the other peoples of the world as against force and selfish aggression. All the peoples of the world are in effect partners in this interest, and for our own part we see very clearly that unless justice be done to others it will not be done to us. The program of the world's peace, therefore, is our program; and that program, the only possible program, as we see it, is this:

I. Open covenants of peace, openly arrived at, after which there shall be no private international understandings of any kind but diplomacy shall proceed always frankly and in the public view.

II. Absolute freedom of navigation upon the seas [...]

III. The removal, so far as possible, of all economic barriers and the establishment of an equality of trade conditions among all the nations [...]

IV. National armaments ...reduced to the lowest point consistent with domestic safety.

V. A free, open-minded, and absolutely impartial adjustment of all colonial claims, based upon a strict observance of the principle that in determining all such questions of sovereignty the interests of the populations concerned must have equal weight with the equitable claims of the government whose title is to be determined.

VI. The evacuation of all Russian territory and [...] a sincere welcome into the society of free nations under institutions of her own choosing [...]

VII. Belgium [...] must be evacuated and restored [...]

VIII. All French territory should be freed and the invaded portions restored, and the wrong done to France by Prussia in 1871 in the matter of Alsace-Lorraine, which has unsettled the peace of the world for nearly fifty years, should be righted [...]

IX. A readjustment of the frontiers of Italy should be effected along clearly recognizable lines of nationality.

X. The peoples of Austria-Hungary [...] should be accorded the freest opportunity to autonomous development.

XI. Rumania, Serbia, and Montenegro should be evacuated [...]

XII. The Turkish portion of the present Ottoman Empire should be assured a secure sovereignty, but the other nationalities which are now under Turkish rule should be assured an undoubted security of life and an absolutely unmolested opportunity of autonomous development [...]

XIII. An independent Polish state should be erected which should include the territories inhabited by indisputably Polish populations, which should be assured a free and secure access to the sea [...]

XIV. A general association of nations must be formed under specific covenants for the purpose of affording mutual guarantees of political independence and territorial integrity to great and small states alike.

[...] For such arrangements and covenants we are willing to fight and to continue to fight until they are achieved [...] We have no jealousy of German greatness, and there is nothing in this program that impairs it. We grudge her no achievement or distinction of learning or of pacific enterprise such as have made her record very bright and very enviable. We do not wish to injure her or to block in any way her legitimate influence or power. We do not wish to fight her either with arms or with hostile arrangements of trade if she is willing to associate herself with us and the other peace-loving nations of the world in covenants of justice and law and fair dealing. We wish her only to accept a place of equality among the peoples of the world, -- the new world in which we now live, -- instead of a place of mastery.

http://net.lib.byu.edu/~rdh7/wwi/1918/14points.html

4.2 Versailles and After: Weimar Foreign Policy in Perspective

The regulations in the Treaty of Versailles, especially the fact that Germany had to accept sole responsibility for the outbreak of WW I, met with very strong opposition in Germany. Historians have argued for a long time about the question whether, or to what extent, the Treaty of Versailles contributed to the takeover of power by the National Socialists and to the outbreak of WW II.

At the time the treaty was signed voices were already being raised concerning the effects on Germany and the Germans of, for example, the reparations regulations. Among these voices were those of Jan Smuts and of the chief economist in the British delegation at Versailles, John Maynard Keynes.

The allies did not want Germany to be one of the initial members of the League of Nations. Germany was to be isolated. So, one of the prime aims of German foreign policy had to be the attempt to overcome this isolation as soon as possible. Against that background one can take a look at the treaties with Russia, an equally isolated country. Foreign Minister Gustav Stresemann took steps to lead Germany out of isolation and into the League of Nations (1926) by implementing his policy of fulfillment. In this era the question of reparations was taken up again and the Dawes-Plan (1924) envisaged a substantial and immediate reduction of those payments. In 1925, by signing the Treaty of Locarno, Germany fulfilled the pre-conditions for being admitted as a full member to the League of Nations (1926). Stresemann who together with Aristide Briant became a 1926 Nobel Peace Laureate is a highly appraised statesman in Germany but in Britain and America there are critical views that even see in him someone paving the way for National Socialism.

M1 General Jan Smuts, Letter to Lloyd George, 26 March 1919

Jan Christian Smuts (1870–1950) was a South African politician and general. He was Prime Minister of South Africa 1919–1924 and 1939–1948. In WW I Smuts was a member of the British War Cabinet, in WW II he served as a Field Marshal. Smuts took part in the Versailles peace negotiations and signed the treaty.

[...] I am seriously afraid that the peace to which we are working is an impossible peace, conceived on a wrong basis; that it will not be accepted by Germany, and, even if accepted, that it will prove utterly unstable, and only serve to promote the anarchy which is rapidly overtaking Europe [...]

To my mind certain points seem quite clear and elementary:

1. We cannot destroy Germany without destroying Europe;
2. We cannot save Europe without the co-operation of Germany.

Yet we are now preparing a peace which must destroy Germany, and yet we think we shall save Europe by so doing! The fact is, the Germans are, have been, and will continue to be, the dominant factor in the Continent of Europe, and no permanent peace is possible which is not based on that fact. The statesmen of the Vienna Congress were wiser in their generation; they looked upon France as necessary to Europe. And yet we presume to look down upon them and their work! My fear is that the Paris Conference may prove one of the historic failures of the world; that the statesmen connected with it will return to their countries broken, discredited men, and that the Bolshevists will reap where they have *sown* [...]

Take again the territorial terms we are preparing. I note that Danzig, an ancient German town with a German population, has to be handed over to Poland together with some millions of Germans, some of them in solid blocks of old Prussian territory. It is rumoured that in addition to Alsace-Lorraine the Saar Valley is also going to France; and that Germany is to be further dismembered by the constitution of a separate state west of the Rhine. I am simply amazed at all this. Are we in our sober senses, or suffering from shell-shock? What has become of Wilson's Fourteen Points, or of your repeated declarations against the humiliation and dismemberment of Germany? I note the stand you have made against some of these things; but that is not enough. We shall be judged, not by our protests, but by our acts.

All these territorial arrangements I look upon as most dangerous, and indeed fatal from the point of view of securing present and future peace. If the Germans are like the rest of us they simply will not accept such terms, and will throw back on their despoilers the responsibility for the resulting chaos. And for the future there is the legacy of revenge.

The fact is, neither Poland nor Bohemia will be politically possible without German goodwill and assistance. They ought to be established on a basis which will secure German co-operation in their future success; and Germany ought to undertake definite liabilities in the peace treaty to assist and protect them militarily and otherwise against Russia and Hungary and against each other. Instead of dismembering and destroying Germany, she ought in a measure to be taken into the scope of our policy, and be made responsible for part of the burden which is clearly too heavy for us to hear. Are we going to defend Poland and Bohemia as we have defended the Ukraine against the Bolshevists? If it is necessary for Germany to be made to hear her share of the heavy burden of the new Europe, she ought not to be despoiled and treated as an international pariah, but rather to be taken in hand by the Allies and helped to her feet again. Unless this is done, I fear we are ploughing the sands of the sea at this Conference. Without German goodwill, neither Poland nor Bohemia will show any stable vitality, and they will become simply problems and burdens for the future politics of Europe [...]

My view is that, in trying to break Germany in order to create and territorially satisfy these smaller States, we are labouring at a task which is bound to fail. We shall get no peace treaty now, and Europe will know no peace hereafter. And in the coming storms these new States will themselves be the first to founder. It is not through breaking Germany that we shall save them; but, on the contrary, they can only be saved by Germany sharing with us the responsibility for their defence and maintenance. But in that case, Poland will have to be satisfied with rights of way to the Baltic, instead of annexing German territory.

I do not know how it stands with the two important questions of punishment for war crimes and exaction of reparations. Here too, however, I would look at the matter from a large point of view, and not ask the impossible. In particular a large indemnity should only be asked on our promise to supply raw materials to re-start German industry. While such a promise would probably induce Germany to accept the liability to pay a very large sum, payment could only be made if German industry is put in a position to supply the goods.

To conclude: even at this late hour I would urge that we revise our attitude towards Germany, and, while making her pay heavily, and also making her undertake burdens for the defence and assistance of Central Europe which we have neither the men nor the means to undertake ourselves, treat her in a different spirit from that in which our proposals have so far been framed; avoid all appearance of dismembering her or subjecting her to indefinite economic servitude and pauperism, and make her join the League of Nations from the beginning. Her complete economic exhaustion and disarmament would prevent her from becoming a military or naval danger in this generation, and her appeasement now may have the effect of turning her into a bulwark against the oncoming Bolshevism of Eastern Europe. [...] I fear, I greatly fear our present panic policy towards Germany will bring failure on this Conference, and spell ruin for Europe. Yours very sincerely,

William Keith Hancock and Jan van der Pool (eds), Selections from the Smuts Papers, Cambridge University Press, 1966, pp. 83–87, taken from: Arthur Marwick and Wendy Simpson eds.,Total War and Social Change 1914–1955, Primary Sources 2, The Open University, Oxford 2001, pp. 62–64.

M2 The Economic Consequences of the Peace by John Maynard Keynes, 1919

Keynes (1883–1946) was chief economic advisor to the British delegation at Versailles and became one of the most influential economists of the 20th century.

Chapter 1: Introductory

[...] Moved by insane delusion and reckless self-regard, the German people overturned the foundations on which we all lived and built. But the spokesmen of the French and British peoples have run the risk of completing the ruin which Germany began, by a peace which, if it is carried into effect, must impair yet further, when it might have restored, the delicate, complicated organisation, already shaken and broken by war, through which alone the European peoples can employ themselves and live. [...]

France, Germany, Italy, Austria, and Holland, Russia and Roumania and Poland, throb together, and their structure and civilisation are essentially one. They flourished together, they have rocked together in a war which we, in spite of our enormous contributions and sacrifices (like though in a less degree than America), economically stood outside, and they may fall together.

In this lies the destructive significance of the Peace of Paris. If the European civil war is to end with France and Italy abusing their momentary victorious power to destroy Germany and Austria-Hungary now prostrate, they invite their own destruction also, being so deeply and inextricably intertwined with their victims by hidden psychic and economic bonds. [...]

Chapter 3: The Conference

[Clemenceau's] principles for the peace can be expressed simply. In the first place, he was a foremost believer in the view of German psychology that the German understands and can understand nothing but intimidation, that he is without generosity or remorse in negotiation, that there is no advantage he will not take of you, and no extent to which he will not demean himself for profit, that he is without honour, pride, or mercy. Therefore you must never negotiate with a German or

conciliate him; you must dictate to him. On no other terms will he respect you, or will you prevent him from cheating you. [...]
So far as possible, therefore, it was the policy of France to set the clock back and to undo what, since 1870, the progress of Germany had accomplished. By loss of territory and other measures her population was to be curtailed; but chiefly the economic system, upon which she depended for her new strength, the vast fabric built upon iron, coal, and transport, must be destroyed. If France could seize, even in part, what Germany was compelled to drop, the inequality of strength between the two rivals for European hegemony might be remedied for many generations.
[...] My purpose in this book is to show that the Carthaginian peace is not practically right or possible.

John Maynard Keynes, The Economic Consequences of the Peace (New York: Harcourt Brace Jovanovich, 1920); taken from:http://socserv2.socsci.mcmaster.ca/~econ/ugcm/3ll3/keynes/peace.htm

M3 The Crisis of 1923 in Perspective

A Comparative View: Extracts from an English and a German Textbook

A) From 1919 Weimar governments faced a growing budget deficit. The insecure Weimar governments opted for inflationary policies. This contributed to the hyperinflation crisis of 1923.
Thus, though in 1923 most Germans blamed the economic crisis on the French and British demands for reparations, in many ways German governments were responsible. In some respects the government actually favoured inflation, since it reduced the real burden of its internal debt – interest and debt repayments on money borrowed from its citizens. (Reparations were payable in gold or goods so their real value would not be affected by inflation.) Modest inflation can be beneficial to stimulate an economy...
The governments continued to print money. By 1923, 300 paper mills and 2,000 printing firms, including newspaper firms, were working 24-hour shifts to produce money. The government needed money to pay compensation to war victims and to those who had lost land under the Treaty of Versailles. It also needed to pay wages to civil servants, welfare benefits and subsidies and provide cheap credit to help industry readjust and maintain full employment. Another factor was the hope that continuing economic problems would reinforce the argument that Germany could not pay reparations and so influence Allied governments to lower the level of their demands.
Foreign governments must also share some of the blame for the crisis. The French and Belgian occupation of the Ruhr in January 1923 came as the final blow to the faltering mark. Sixty thousand troops took control of all industries and railways in order to seize resources in lieu of payments that were overdue. However, it was not so much the invasion itself as the government's response to it that let loose hyperinflation. The governments called for passive resistance, that no one should cooperate with the invaders. Civil servants, miners and others went on strike, financed by the government. In places resistance was far from passive and over 140 Germans were killed in clashes with French troops. Revenues to the government fell as Germany's industrial heartland was disrupted but expenditure on welfare increased rapidly, again funded by increased printing of money.

Hite, John/Hinton, Chris: Weimar and Nazi Germany, John Murray, London 2000, p. 49;

B) Reparationsverpflichtungen
Mit Reichskanzler Wirth und Außenminister Walter Rathenau änderte sich die deutsche Reparationspolitik von Grund auf. Nach den Vorstellungen der beiden Politiker sollte Deutschland bis an die Grenzen seiner Leistungsfähigkeit versuchen, die Reparationen zu erfüllen, um gerade dadurch ihre Unerfüllbarkeit deutlich zu machen. Diese von den Rechtsparteien heftig bekämpfte Erfüllungspolitik scheiterte an der unnachgiebigen Haltung Frankreichs. Der konservative Ministerpräsident Raymond Poincaré wollte die Reparationsfrage dazu benutzen, das Ruhrgebiet in seine Hände zu bekommen. und nach

Möglichkeit entlang dem Rhein eine neue Grenze zwischen Frankreich und Deutschland zu ziehen.

Besetzung des Ruhrgebiets und passiver Widerstand

Im Dezember 1922 befand sich Deutschland mit seinen Lieferungen bei Holz und Kohle geringfügig im Rückstand. Poincaré benutzte dies als Vorwand, um am 11. Januar 1923 60000 französische und belgische Soldaten ins Ruhrgebiet einmarschieren zu lassen. Eine Gruppe französischer Beamter und Ingenieure sollte die deutsche Kohle- und Stahlproduktion kontrollieren und die strikte Einhaltung der Lieferungsverpflichtungen sicherstellen.

Die empörte Bevölkerung war bereit, sich mit allen Mitteln zur Wehr zu setzen. Sämtliche Reparationslieferungen wurden sofort eingestellt, Beamte und Bevölkerung von der Reichsregierung zum „passiven Widerstand“ gegen die Besatzungsbehörden aufgerufen. Doch schon bald mussten die Menschen immer größere Entbehrungen auf sich nehmen. Außerdem erschöpfte sich die Leistungsfähigkeit Deutschlands: Im September 1923 kostete der Ruhrkampf das Reich täglich 40 Millionen Goldmark.

Die sprunghaft gestiegenen Ausgaben ließen sich nicht durch Einnahmen decken, wieder mussten die Notenpressen das Defizit im Reichshaushalt ausgleichen.

Der Tauschhandel war an der Tagesordnung, das Geld hatte seine Funktion als Wertmesser verloren. Der Währungszusammenbruch traf alle, die ihre Ersparnisse auf Konten angelegt hatten, vor allem die Rentner und die kleinbürgerliche Schicht der Beamten und Angestellten. Die Besitzer von Sachwerten erlitten durch die Inflation kaum Verluste, oft konnten sie sogar Gewinne erzielen, wenn sie aufgenommene Kredite mit entwertetem Geld zurückzahlten. Gewinner der Inflation war auch der größte Schuldner, das Reich. […]

Am 13. August 1923 bildete Gustav Stresemann eine Regierung der „Großen Koalition“ (SPD, DDP, Zentrum, DVP). Er brach am 26. September den sinnlos gewordenen Widerstand im Ruhrgebiet ab und ordnete die Wiederaufnahme der Reparationsleistungen an Frankreich und Belgien an. Poincaré hatte auf der bedingungslosen Kapitulation bestanden.

Hein-Mooren, Klaus Dieter, u.a.: Von der Französischen Revolution bis zum Nationalsozialismus, Buchners Verlag, Bamberg 1992, S. 321–323.

M4 Letter from Gustav Stresemann to the former German Crown Prince, September 1925

Gustav Stresemann (1878–1929), co-founder of the liberal-right German People's Party (DVP) in 1918, was Chancellor in 1923, and Foreign Minister 1923–1929

In my opinion there are three great tasks which confront German foreign policy in the immediate future.

In the first place the solution of the reparations question in a way acceptable to Germany, and the assurance of peace.

Secondly the protection of Germans abroad, those 10 to 12 million of our kindred who now live under a foreign yoke in foreign lands.

The third is the readjustment of our eastern frontiers; the recovery of Danzig, the Polish corridor, and a correction of the frontier in Upper Silesia.

Hence the Locarno Pact which guarantees us peace and makes England, as well as Italy, guarantors of our western frontiers.

I would utter a warning against any ideas of flirting with Bolshevism; we cannot involve ourselves in an alliance with Russia though an understanding is possible on another basis. When the Russians are in Berlin, the red flag will at once be flown from the castle, and in Russia, where they hope for a world revolution, there will be much joy at the spread of Bolshevism as far as the Elbe. The most important thing for German policy is the liberation of German soil from any occupying force. On that account German policy must be one of finesse and avoidance of great decisions.

E. Sutton, Gustav Stresemann, His Diaries, Letters and Papers (Macmillan, 1935, adapted))

M5 Jessie Lewis: Gustav Stresemann – Advocate of International Understanding or Precursor of the Nazi Assault (1988)

Stresemann, before he took office, had inscribed on the program of Deutsche Volkspartei the "abolition" of the Treaty of Versailles and his substitution on his accession to power of the catchword "fulfillment" was merely a disguise for those sapping and mining operations against the Treaty which he initiated with the demand for withdrawal of the Control Commission and the evacuation of the Rhineland. Relying upon Germany's importance in Europe, and thinking in terms of international trade, he believed that the victorious powers could not easily afford to ignore or even destroy her. The price exacted by Stresemann for the Locarno Pact was not only the withdrawal of the Control Commission, but silence. He got it. It became "bad form" for any one to question whether Germany was, or was not, in a state of grace in the matter of disarmament. […]

To assure a rapid return of defeated Germany to a position of first rank, he was prepared to utilize the resources of the young Soviet Republic and advised that friendly relations be maintained with the Bolsheviks. Stresemann skillfully used Germany's entry into the League both to increase his options toward the Soviet Union and to intensify German pressure on France for parity in armaments. Moscow took the hint and within a year of Locarno, in April 1926, a treaty of neutrality between the Soviet Union and Germany was signed in Berlin. Having opted for the West and for democracy in 1919, Germany could regard herself as having been rebuffed by the West at Versailles. It was natural to reconsider the other option, alignment with Russia, without accepting communism. As a dissatisfied "revisionist" power, Russia could regard the League of Nations as an organization of the victors alone. The celebrated Treaty of Rapallo (1922) between Germany and Russia reflects this attitude.

France had no objection prior to the world war to concluding an alliance with the autocratically governed Russia of the Tsars, in spite of the democratic and republican form of her government and the constitutional differences between the two countries. The attitude of the French was a very sensible one from the point of view of their own interests. Similarly, Germany likewise cannot be blamed if today she is anxious to establish cordial economic and political relations with Soviet Russia.

Stresemann, 1st April 1926, broadcast address regarding the Treaty of Berlin.[…]

Stresemann had not abandoned nationalism, but was determined to pursue it realistically, in the tradition of Bismarck, not after the fashion in which he had once been a fanatical annexationist. One of the few things the men of Locarno agreed on during the first half of 1926 was the desirability of conducting negotiations by means of informal and secret meetings of the Locarno foreign ministers held during sessions of the League Council: "the Geneva tea parties." […] When Stresemann's papers became available, they seemed to contradict the benign estimation of him. They revealed a calculating practitioner of Realpolitik who pursued the traditional German national interest with ruthless persistence. For Stresemann, these interests were straightforward: to restore Germany to its pre-1914 stature, to dispose of the financial burdens of reparations, to attain military parity with France and Great Britain, to revise Germany's Eastern border, and to achieve the union (Anschluss) of Austria and Germany. Kissinger concluded that Stresemann was therefore not a "good European" in the post-World War II sense of the phrase but it would be more accurate to view Nazi excesses as an interruption of Stresemann's gradual and almost certainly peaceful progression of achieving a decisive role for his country in Europe. Stresemann died in 1929, a year in which Germany was suddenly confronted by economic catastrophe. Meanwhile, lurking in the background, and preparing to take advantage of any such change of fortune, were Hitler and the Nazis.

http://userwww.sfsu.edu/~epf/2000/lewis.html

4.3 Germany at the End of the Weimar Republic

The Great Depression had a devastating effect on all industrialized countries. Germany was hard-hit by an economic slump and massive unemployment. Politically this was the period of the Presidential Cabinets, based on §48 of the Weimar Constitution, i.e. on government by decree – leading up to the Nazi Party's rise to power.

M1 Germany in Despair

Excerpt from the speech by von Papen, German Chancellor, to the Lausanne Conference of 16 June–9 July 1932. Franz von Papen (1879–1969), Zentrum politician, Chancellor in 1932 (Presidential cabinet) and Vice-Chancellor in the first Hitler cabinet, 1933/34)

The desperate situation which prevails today is evidenced by the number of 2,5 million unemployed […] In Germany this state of things has most strongly shaken the confidence of the masses in the good functioning of the capitalist system. […]

The German situation is characterized by the following:

1. The high level of interest, which crushes agriculture and also industry;
2. The burden of taxation, which is so oppressive, in the opinion of the Special Advisory Committee, that it cannot be increased, but has yet been increased, in order to assure the very existence of the State, by the imposition of fresh taxes within the last few days;
3. The external debt, the service of which becomes ever more difficult by reason of the progressive diminution of the surplus of exports; and
4. Unemployment, which is relatively more widespread than in any other country whatever, and which constitutes from 20 to as per cent of the population a burden on public funds.

- What is particularly fatal is that an ever-growing number of young people have no possibility and no hope of finding employment and earning their livelihood. Despair and the political radicalization of the youthful section of the population are the consequences of this state of things […]
- The former reserves of the Reichsbank are exhausted. […]
- The external debt of Germany, with its very heavy interest charges, is, for the most part, attributable to the transfers of capital and the withdrawals of credits which have been the consequences of the execution of the Treaty of Versailles and of the reparations agreements. […]
- Public and private economy are today […] devoid of any reserves and find themselves faced with an unemployment problem unprecedented in history.

Documents on British Foreign Policy, Second series, vol. 3, 197–201
taken from: http://www.mtholyoke.edu/acad/intrel/papen.htm

M2 Peace on Earth

Reparation payments had been a major issue since the Treaty of Versailles. Neither the Dawes Plan nor the Young Plan had provided a long-term viable solution to the problem. In view of the economic crisis and the international financial and economic problems a conference was held in Lausanne in 1932.

"Peace on Earth. ..." ... [T]he motives and emotions of the statesmen at Lausanne last week did them credit. So many conferences since the War have ended in nothing at all. It was an historic moment when the Chancellor of Germany, having battled the whole night for a clause wiping out what his people call the "War guilt lie," finally gave in at 3 p.m. saying: […]

If the Lausanne agreement is ratified by Great Britain, France, Germany, Japan, Italy and Belgium – a very big IF – the outstanding achievement will be to reduce German Reparations by 99 %, to a payment of 1 ¢ to $ 1.

Naturally not all this scaling down was done by the Lausanne Conference. The process began soon after the late Baron Cunliffe, onetime Governor of the Bank of England (1913–1918), officially informed Prime Minister David Lloyd George in 1919 that Germany could pay 116 billion dollars. This was a statement so obviously absurd that a year later the Boulogne Conference tentatively set 64 billions as what is usually considered the "original sum" of Germany's debt in Reparations.

One year later the Germans, through President Harding, offered to pay 48 billions on condition that some of their surrendered territories be returned. This offer the Allies spurned. A few days later, in April 1921, the Reparations Commission decided that 32 billions would be "fair."

This was followed by the Dawes Plan that Germany pay 595 millions per annum for an indefinite number of years (1924). Great feature of the ensuing Young Plan was that it purported to fix 58½ years definitely as the time over which Germany would be required to pay a total of some 27 billions (TIME, June 10, 1929). [...]

The Lausanne settlement is supposed to provide for repayment of these bonds and scales down Reparations to a final total of only 714 millions–1 ¢ each on the original 64 billion dollars of 1920 which was in itself a cut of nearly 50% from the Governor of the Bank of England's first fantastic figure of 116 billions. [...]

In Berlin 25,000 brownshirts jeered what fascist orators called "von Papen's incomprehensible weakness." "This treaty," summed up Adolf Hitler, "will not be worth more than three marks (71 ¢) inside of six months."

The Hearst of Germany, her famed "Little Man In Blue," Dr. Alfred Hugenberg, turned his Nationalist press, which originally supported Chancellor von Papen, against him. Only the German Socialists, and they only because they are Internationalists, wholeheartedly supported von Papen. The Chancellor who recently suppressed the Socialist Vorwärts for five days for publishing a scurrilous cartoon (TIME, July 11), was praised for his work at Lausanne in the first issue of Vorwärts to appear last week.

TIME, Monday, Jul. 18, 1932;

taken from: http://www.time.com/time/magazine/article/0,9171,753379,00.html

4.4 Nazi Germany and the U.S. Looking at Each Other

Early in 1933 we see a new administration in both Germany and the United States, both promising to overcome the economic problems of the Great Depression and both promising to do even more, i.e. to lead their countries into a modern new era.

From very early on after the Nazi Party's rise to power Americans looked rather skeptically at Germany. They soon came to the conclusion that the disconcerting news and developments were not just a Nazi aberration but that there was something fundamentally wrong with the Germans and their heritage. Numerous publications inquired into the German national character. Book titles like 'German Schizophrenia' and 'Is Germany Incurable' show that the Germans were considered to be suffering from a fundamental illness. By the end of the war this approach resulted in the Morgenthau-Plan which proposed the total de-industrialization of Germany and which for a short period in 1944 was part of official U.S. policy. Germany was looked at rather like a patient – to be treated by a psychotherapist, namely by the international community.

From Germany's point of view the United States were to be acknowledged in regard to their economic strength and their technological progress, but in all other regards the view was negative. Nazi Germany saw U.S. society as embodying cultural degeneration.

M1 The Consul General in Berlin (Messersmith) to the Under Secretary of State (Phillips), BERLIN, November 23, 1933

DEAR MR. PHILLIPS:

In spite of the way in which the feelings of the German people have been whipped up by this new Government I do not believe that the majority of the German people yet desire war, but there is certainly no great desire for peace. Everything that is being done in the country to-day has for its object to make the people believe that Germany is threatened vitally in every aspect of its life by outside influences and by other countries. Everything is being done to use this feeling to stimulate military training and exercises, and innumerable measures are being taken to develop the German people into a hardy, sturdy race which will be able to meet all comers. The military spirit is constantly growing. It cannot be otherwise. The leaders of Germany to-day have no desire for peace unless it is a peace which the world makes at the expense of complete compliance with German desires and ambitions. Hitler and his associates really and sincerely want peace for the moment, but only to have a chance to get ready to use force if it is found finally essential. They are preparing their way so carefully that these is not in my mind any question but that the German people will be with them when they want to use force and when they feel that they have the necessary means to carry through their objects.

Just what Germany will do on the disarmament question I think it is too early to definitely predict, but that she has a definite aim which she will go after unswervingly, we can take for granted. She will fight shy of all conferences, but will make constant overtures all around and constant protestations of a desire to cooperate and of a will for peace. Germany will particularly embarrass France by protestations of her willingness to do all sorts of things, with the hope of making trouble between France and England and the United States. It will I believe be exceedingly difficult to pin her down to anything. In the meantime she will go on rearming. This is what he wants to do and will do. Germany may make all sorts of protestations with regard to the reduction of armaments by other countries, but what she is interested in is not so much the other countries cutting down their armaments, as having a free hand or rather time to go ahead and rearm herself.

Cordially and sincerely yours,

GEORGE S. MESSERSMITH

Source: U.S., Department of State, Publication 1983, Peace and War: United States Foreign Policy, 1931–1941 (Washington, D.C.: U.S., Government Printing Office, 1943, p. 195.

M2 The Appointed Minister to Austria (Messersmith) to the Under Secretary of State (Phillips)

Transmitting a Memorandum to the Embassy on the "Main Purpose of the Nazis," written by Douglas Miller, the Acting Commercial Attache, 21 April 1934

The fundamental purpose is to secure a greater share of the world's future for the Germans, the expansion of German territory and growth of the German race until it constitutes the largest and most powerful nation in the world, and ultimately, according to some Nazi leaders, until it dominates the entire globe.

The German people suffering from a traditional inferiority complex, smarting from their defeat in the war and the indignities of the post-war period, disillusioned in their hopes of a speedy return to prosperity along traditional lines, inflamed by irresponsible demagogic slogans and flattered by the statement that their German racial inheritance gives them inherent superior rights over other peoples, have to a large measure adopted the National Socialist point of view for the time being.

ECONOMIC AIMS

There are two other purposes subsidiary to the main purpose. Germany is to be made the economic center of a self-sustaining territorial block whose dependent nations in Central and Eastern Europe will look to Berlin for leadership. This block is to be so constituted that it can defy wartime blockade and be large enough to give the peoples in it the benefits of free trade now enjoyed by the 48 American States. In accordance with this purpose, an agricultural self-sufficiency program has been adopted, foreign foodstuffs are being rigorously excluded or the imported supply secured in increasing quantities from Central and Southeastern Europe. A hereditary peasantry has been set up, firmly attached to the soil through the prohibition of the sale or mortgaging of the peasants' land or crops. An increasing number of commodities have been placed under Government monopolies with fixed prices to consumers and producers, the principle of the numerus clausus or fixed number of persons engaged in any occupation has been increasingly adopted. The National Socialist conception of the correct or Government-fixed price instead of the price fixed by supply and demand has been introduced.

SOCIAL AIMS

The second subsidiary purpose is the welding of all individuals in the present and future Greater Germany into a homogeneous racial family, gladly obedient to the will of its leader, with class and cultural differences inside the country eliminated, but a sharp line drawn between Germans and the foreign world outside. In carrying out this purpose, the Jews are to be entirely eliminated, the Slavic or eastern elements in the population to be minimized and eventually bred out of the race. A national religion is in process of organization; trade unions, political parties and all social, political, cultural, trade or other organizations not affiliated with the National Socialist party, have been abolished, the individual's rights have been largely taken away. In the future the nation is to count for everything, the individual for nothing. Germany is to engage in a gigantic struggle with the rest of the world to grow at the expense of its neighbors. The German population owes the nation the patriotic duty of supporting it and bringing forward all necessary sacrifices to reach the common goal.

RETENTION OF POWER

To these long-distance objectives must be added the fourth and most important purpose of all, namely to retain control at all costs. The National Socialist party may compromise on distant objectives, if necessary, but cannot compromise on a question of retaining its absolute hold on the German people. This control had been gained by making most irresponsible and extravagant promises; by the studied use of the press, the radio, public meetings, parades, flags, uniforms, and all methods of working on popular psychology and finally by the use of force. This control once lost, could never be regained. It is absolutely necessary for the party to continue to make a show of success and to keep popular enthusiasm and fanaticism alive. There must be no open criticism or grumbling, even discussion of the future form of the State, the form in which industry is to be organized, or the laws regarding the hereditary peasantry is prohibited. Since the German public is politically inept and unusually docile, the Nazi movement has been able to dominate the situation for the past year, but the hard facts of the economic situation are beginning to be felt by the more intelligent Germans, particularly bankers, business men, professional men and persons who have touch with the outside world.

DANGER OF WAR

The Nazis are not satisfied with the existing map of Europe. They are at heart belligerent and aggressive. True, they desire nothing more than a period of peace for several years in which they can gradually re-arm and discipline their people. This period may be years, 10 years, or longer, but the more completely their experiments succeed the more certain is a large-scale war in Europe some day.

NAZIS WANT TO WIPE OUT 1918

In estimating the aims and purposes of the National Socialist movement, we must not make the mistake of putting too much reliance on public statements designed for consumption abroad which breathe the spirit of good peace and will and assert the intention of the Government to promote the welfare of the German people and good relations with their neighbors. Nor should we imagine that the present Government leaders will feel and act as we would in their circumstances, namely think only of Germany's welfare. The real emotional drive behind the Nazi program is not so much love of their own country as dislike of other countries. The Nazis will never be content in merely promoting the welfare of the German people. They desire to be feared and envied by foreigners and to wipe out the memory of 1918 by inflicting humiliations in particular upon the French, the Poles, the Czechs and anybody else they can get their hands on.

A careful examination of Hitler's book and his public speeches reveals the fact that he cannot be considered as absolutely sane and normal on this subject. The same is true of many other Nazi leaders. They have capitalized the wounded inferiority complex of the German people, and magnified their own bitter feelings into a cult of dislike against the foreign world which is past the bounds of ordinary good sense and reason. Let us repeat this fact and let it sink in, the National Socialist movement is building a tremendous military machine, physically very poorly armed, but morally aggressive and belligerent. The control of this machine lies in the hands of narrow, ignorant and unscrupulous adventurers who have been slightly touched with madness from brooding over Germany's real or imagined wrongs, as well as the slights and indignities thrown in their own individual way as they attempted to organize the movement. Power of this kind concentrated in hands like these is dangerous. The Nazis are determined to secure more power and more territory in Europe. If this is voluntarily given to them by peaceful means, well and good, but if not, they will certainly use force. That is the only meaning behind the manifold activities of the movement in Germany today

Douglas Miller.

U.S., Department of State, Publication 1983, Peace and War: United States Foreign Policy, 1931–1941 (Washington, D.C.: U.S., Government Printing Office, 1943, pp. 211–214.

M3 Prescription for Germany

Time Magazine, Monday, 14 May 1945

Like everybody else, scientists have been brooding about the problem of what to do with Germany. Like everybody else, they have various opinions. But one group of them has produced a plan to submit to the State Department. Its ambitious aim: to change "the German character."

Diagnosis. Gathered together by Richard M. Brickner, author of Is Germany Incurable?, the 30 eminent consultants include Freudian Psychoanalyst Franz Alexander, Anthropologist Margaret Mead, Psychiatrist Adolf Meyer, Psychologist Gardner Murphy, Physician Alvan L. Barach. After long pondering, they concluded that the German people have been suffering (for more than a century) from a bad case of "psychocultural aggressiveness."

Symptoms. How did the German people get that way? The scientists' answer: German traditions and institutions have bred into the individual German an aggressive concern about his "status" or position. In the family, the father has long been absolute master, sternly dominating his wife and children. Business, the professions, politics and education have likewise been ruled by an authoritarian system in which, to assert and defend his status, a German bullies his inferiors, kowtows to his superiors. "The German alternately commands and scrapes." Unlike Americans and Englishmen, who consider it unsporting to exert their full strength against weaker opponents, Germans are traditionally most brutal and ruthless toward their inferiors. In their relations with other nations, they have been alternately arrogant and afflicted with a persecution complex, a condition resembling paranoia.

Uprooting. From this diagnosis, the group deduced that it would be useless merely to preach democracy to the German people: they are emotionally incapable of understanding the democratic principles of give & take and cooperation among equals. Suggesting a "stern" peace rather than a "hard" one, they proposed a complete uprooting of the institutions which have been the sources of Germany's infection.

Many a scientist who disagrees with the blanket diagnosis may nonetheless agree with most of the group's proposals. Items:

Total defeat of the Wehrmacht, "for over a century ... the sinew of German pride." This operation, now accomplished, lays a psychological basis for a cure.

Stern trial and punishment, not only of the top Nazis but to "extend down vertically into the population for a certain distance." To be executed: all high Nazi and Gestapo officials, Gauleiters, members of the Army High Command who helped to mistreat occupied countries, lesser officials who zealously carried out Nazi policies. To be imprisoned for life: all smaller fry who acted with "singular cruelty." To be interned, exiled or held in labor battalions: all incurable antidemocrats.

Abolition, for perhaps two generations, of Germany's sovereignty.

Decentralization (but not dismemberment) of German government, industry, schools, cultural institutions (e.g., music festivals, sports, etc.).

Allied administration for an indefinite period of all German international communications (radio, shipping, aviation, etc.).

A buildup of the prestige of German women, who should be given the chief role in handling relief and education.

A long-term program to train the German people in the advantages of democracy by education, economic planning, political reform. Trustworthy Germans should be found to lead these reforms. A genuine German revolution should be encouraged.

taken from: http://www.time.com/time/magazine/printout/0,8816,792120,00.html

M4 Our Polemics against the USA

The Nazi Party depended heavily on speakers to get its message across. Those speakers needed to be informed. The following is a translation of instructions to speakers in February 1942, shortly after the U.S. entered the war. What should be said about the U.S., and what arguments should be avoided? The material was labeled "Very Confidential!", although there was not all that much secret in it.

Recently, inappropriate arguments have often been used against the USA. The primary argument we want to make is that it displays a complete lack of culture. Many examples of life in the States provide clear proof of this. For example, the ridiculous glorification of film stars shows a general lack of truly inspiring ideas. Further proof of the cultural deficiencies of this nation is provided by the wild sensationalism evident in such disgusting things as women boxers, mud wrestling matches, freak shows, coverage of particularly terrible criminals, and so on. In view of these facts, we are unwilling to give its president the right to point a finger at Germany, the country with a highly developed culture that is a thousand years old. This is the main argument to use in dealing with that hypocrite Roosevelt. On the other hand, it is entirely false to ridicule the civilizing development of technology in the United States. *It is not appropriate to argue against the USA* because of the fact that North Americans lust after fast cars and trains, after the best luxury railway cars with bars, film viewing cars, or automobiles with sleeping and cooking facilities. *Using all technological methods is an understandable part of development.*

National Socialism, after all, used technology as much as possible during its fight for power.

The shortage of space along the rocky coast of New York and elsewhere has led to *tall buildings* and *skyscrapers*. *This is not to be evaluated as a perversion of American architecture.* All new and advanced technology leads to new architectural styles. There is nothing wrong with that. *It would be wrong to block progress only because of respect for tradition.*

The decisive point is that these advances find their best examples and greatest success by us in Germany, not in the USA. Germany has the best highways in the world. We build the fastest automobiles. That was proven at the major international auto races before the war. At a race in New York, our vehicles did so well during trial runs that the USA withdrew its own cars from the race. Much of our success in the current war is due to major German developments in using motors on land, water, and in the air,

Germany has the best and most architecturally striking bridges. The buildings erected by the Organisation Todt and the masterpieces of Professor Speer are unique in all the world, including the USA.

German scientists and inventors have developed new materials that were the cause of many jokes and contemptuous commentaries in the USA. Today, the United States has lost its possessions in the Far East, and thereby its economic base. We have good materials that we produce ourselves, while the USA is shocked by the deficiencies of its former economic order.

For these reasons, we have every right energetically to insist that the United States shut its mouth about us and about Europe. The USA has not proven that it has anything to give to the world, neither in scientific developments nor with respect to the intellectual leadership of the American people. The best proof of that is the lack of political instinct that the parties display in abusing the broad masses of the United States. Those masses are further betrayed and lied to by Roosevelt and his Jewish Brain Trust.

We thus reject stupid phrases that reach us and the European public about a coming American Century. The Europeans alone will determine what happens in Europe, and Germany, with its inexhaustible culture, civilization, and achievement, will have the major role.

The source: „Unsere Polemik gegen USA,“ Redner-Schnellinformation, Lieferung 26, 21 February 1942. http://www.calvin.edu/academic/cas/gpa/rsi26.htm

5. The Cold War

The Cold War ended with the dissolution of the Soviet Union in 1991 and with the 'fall of the wall' in Berlin in 1989, which had been a symbol for the bipolar division of the world during the Cold War era. But the Cold War, which derived its name from the policy to avoid direct military conflicts between the two major players, the USA and the USSR, has recently flared up again, not only in political rhetoric regarding disagreements between the USA and Russia but also in the context of the 'war on terrorism' after the devastating attack on the Twin Towers in New York on 9/11.
The Cold War has determined world politics from its early stages in the 1920s, when the USA (in alliance with the other Western European powers) tried to prevent the Bolsheviks' seizure of Power in Russia till the late 1980s. Not until the late 1960s did other nations emerge that were able to free themselves from the power play of the USA and the USSR, that were always trying to win new allies against the enemy, thus proving their own system to be superior. Some nations could even use the superpower's antagonism for their own ends and gained by it. But even if some aspects of the Cold War must be reconsidered, e.g. the role of Third World countries that had not been simple victims and playthings of the powerful but rather politically independent actors in their own right, or even if some questions must remain unanswered, e.g. the question who really started it, it is still safe to say that this conflict had global dimensions and its repercussions can still be felt today. Even more so: its legacies have only started to come to the fore and will pose problems for the foreseeable future.

5.1 From Friends to Cold Warriors – the Ideological Hardening of the Former Allies

M1 Churchill's Iron Curtain Speech and Stalin's Reply, March 1946

Winston Churchill held one of the most famous speeches of the Cold War at Fulton, Missouri, on 6 March 1946; officially entitled the "Sinews of Peace Address" it nevertheless came to be known as the 'Iron Curtain Speech'; despite not being Prime Minister at the time, Churchill's political views had great impact. The Soviet leaders were, not unexpectedly, unhappy with Churchill's speech. Ten days later the Soviet daily newspaper Pravda published an interview in which Stalin criticized the tough rhetoric and criticism of the events unfolding in Eastern Europe.
Although Churchill is not too lively a speaker, this speech is worth listening to if only partially, as his accurate and clear pronunciation makes it easy to follow and thus a good speech to listen to for learners. It is easily available as sound-file or even video-file on the net (e.g.: http://www.americanrhetoric.com/speeches/winstonchurchillsinewsofpeace.htm).

a) Churchill

[...] I have a strong admiration and regard for the valiant Russian people and for my wartime comrade, Marshal Stalin. There is deep sympathy and goodwill in Britain – and I doubt not here also – towards the peoples of all the Russias and a resolve to persevere through many differences and rebuffs in establishing lasting friendships [...] It is my duty however, for I am sure you would wish me to state the facts as I see them to you, to place before you certain facts about the present position in Europe.
From Stettin in the Baltic to Trieste in the Adriatic, an iron curtain has descended across the Continent. Behind that line lie all the capitals of the ancient states of Central and

Eastern Europe. Warsaw, Berlin, Prague, Vienna, Budapest, Belgrade, Bucharest and Sofia, all these famous cities and the populations around them lie in what I must call the Soviet sphere, and all are subject in one form or another, not only to Soviet influence but to a very high and, in many cases, increasing measure of control from Moscow [...] The Communist parties, which were very small in all these Eastern States of Europe, have been raised to preeminence and power far beyond their numbers and are seeking everywhere to obtain totalitarian control. Police governments are prevailing in nearly every case, and so far, except in Czechoslovakia, there is no true democracy [...] Whatever conclusions may be drawn from these facts – and facts they are – this is certainly not the Liberated Europe we fought to build up. Nor is it one which contains the essentials of permanent peace.

[...] I do not believe that Soviet Russia desires war. What they desire is the fruits of war and the indefinite expansion of their power and doctrines. But what we have to consider here today, while time remains, is the permanent prevention of war and the establishment of conditions of freedom and democracy as rapidly as possible in all countries. Our difficulties and dangers will not be removed by closing our eyes to them. They will not be removed by mere waiting to see what happens; nor will they be removed by a policy of appeasement. What is needed is a settlement, and the longer this is delayed, the more difficult it will be and the greater our dangers will become.

From what I have seen of our Russian friends and Allies during the war, I am convinced that there is nothing they admire so much as strength, and there is nothing for which they have less respect than for weakness, especially military weakness. For that reason the old doctrine of a balance of power is unsound. We cannot afford, if we can help it, to work on narrow margins, offering temptations to a trial of strength. If the Western Democracies stand together in strict adherence to the principles of the United Nations Charter, their influence for furthering those principles will be immense and no one is likely to molest them. If however they become divided or falter in their duty and if these all-important years are allowed to slip away, then indeed catastrophe may overwhelm us all [...]

b) Stalin

[...] In substance, Mr. Churchill now stands in the position of a firebrand of war. And Mr. Churchill is not alone here. He has friends not only in England but also in the United States of America.

In this respect, one is reminded remarkably of Hitler and his friends. Hitler began to set war loose by announcing his racial theory, declaring that only people speaking the German language represent a fully valuable nation. Mr. Churchill begins to set war loose, also by a racial theory, maintaining that only nations speaking the English language are fully valuable nations, called upon to decide the destinies of the entire world.

The German racial theory brought Hitler and his friends to the conclusion that the Germans, as the only fully valuable nation, must rule over other nations. The English racial theory brings Mr. Churchill and his friends to the conclusion that nations speaking the English language, being the only fully valuable nations, should rule over the remaining nations of the world [...]

As a result of the German invasion, the Soviet Union has irrevocably lost in battles with the Germans, and also during the German occupation and through the expulsion of Soviet citizens to German slave labor camps, about 7,000,000 people. In other words, the Soviet Union has lost in men several times more than Britain and the United States together.

It may be that some quarters are trying to push into oblivion these sacrifices of the Soviet people which insured the liberation of Europe from the Hitlerite yoke.

But the Soviet Union cannot forget them. One can ask therefore, what can be surprising in the fact that the Soviet Union, in a desire to ensure its security for the future, tries to achieve that these countries should

have governments whose relations to the Soviet Union are loyal? How can one, without having lost one's reason, qualify these peaceful aspirations of the Soviet Union as 'expansionist tendencies' of our Government?
[...] Mr. Churchill wanders around the truth when he speaks of the growth of the influence of the Communist parties in Eastern Europe [...] The growth of the influence of Communism cannot be considered accidental. It is a normal function. The influence of the Communists grew because during the hard years of the mastery of fascism in Europe, Communists showed themselves to be reliable, daring and self-sacrificing fighters against fascist regimes for the liberty of peoples.

Hanhimäki, Jussi (Hrsg.): The Cold War: a History in Documents and Eyewitness Accounts. Oxford: Oxford University Press 2004, S. 47–48.

M2 Kennan's Long Telegram, 1946

As a diplomat in Moscow at the time Georg Forster Kennan (1904–2005) sent a rather 'long telegram' to the US, analyzing in detail the Soviet frame of mind, their official and unofficial policies for the years to come and drew his conclusions in the form of advice on how to react – officially and unofficially. This telegram became very influential and was made public a year later as an article (The Sources of Soviet Conduct) in "Foreign Affairs" which helped to instill US-American anti-Communism even deeper. The Long Telegram may well be worthwhile reading in its entirety, maybe as a group exercise, so that every group works on a different section of the text. The full text of the telegram is easily found on the net, e.g. http://www.gwu.edu/~nsarchiv/coldwar/documents/episode-1/kennan.htm, the article can be found here: http://www.historyguide.org/europe/kennan.html.

The Charge in the Soviet Union (Kennan) to the Secretary of State

SECRET

Moscow, February 22, 1946--9 p.m. [Received February 22--3: 52 p.m.]

511. Answer to Dept's 284, Feb 3 [13] involves questions so intricate, so delicate, so strange to our form of thought, and so important to analysis of our international environment that I cannot compress answers into single brief message without yielding to what I feel would be dangerous degree of over-simplification. I hope, therefore, Dept will bear with me if I submit in answer to this question five parts, subjects of which will be roughly as follows:

(1) Basic features of post-war Soviet outlook.

(2) Background of this outlook

(3) Its projection in practical policy on official level.

(4) Its projection on unofficial level.

(5) Practical deductions from standpoint of US policy.

I apologize in advance for this burdening of telegraphic channel; but questions involved are of such urgent importance, particularly in view of recent events, that our answers to them, if they deserve attention at all, seem to me to deserve it at once. [...]

Part 5: [...] In summary, we have here a political force committed fanatically to the belief that with US there can be no permanent modus vivendi that it is desirable and necessary that the internal harmony of our society be disrupted, our traditional way of life be destroyed, the international authority of our state be broken, if Soviet power is to be secure. This political force has complete power of disposition over energies of one of world's greatest peoples and resources of world's richest national territory, and is borne along by deep and powerful currents of Russian nationalism. In addition, it has an elaborate and far flung apparatus for exertion of its influence in other countries, an apparatus of amazing flexibility and versatility, managed by people whose experience and skill in underground methods are presumably without parallel in history. Finally, it is seemingly inaccessible to considerations of reality in its basic reactions. For it, the vast fund of objective fact about human society is not, as with us, the measure against which outlook is constantly being tested and re-formed, but a grab bag from which individual items are selected arbitrarily and tendenciously to bolster an outlook already preconceived. This is admittedly not a pleasant picture. Problem of how to cope with this force in [is] undoubtedly greatest task our diplomacy has ever faced and probably greatest it will ever have to face. It should be point of departure from which our political general staff work at present juncture should proceed. It should be approached with same thoroughness and care as solution of major strategic problem in war, and if necessary, with no smaller outlay in planning effort. I cannot attempt to suggest all answers here. But I would like to record my conviction that problem is within our power to solve – and that without recourse to any general military conflict. And in support of this conviction there are certain observations of a more encouraging nature I should like to make:

(1) Soviet power, unlike that of Hitlerite Germany […] It does not work by fixed plans. It does not take unnecessary risks. Impervious to logic of reason, and it is highly sensitive to logic of force. For this reason it can easily withdraw--and usually does when strong resistance is encountered at any point. Thus, if the adversary has sufficient force and makes clear his readiness to use it, he rarely has to do so. If situations are properly handled there need be no prestige-engaging showdowns.

(2) Gauged against Western World as a whole, Soviets are still by far the weaker force. Thus, their success will really depend on degree of cohesion, firmness and vigor which Western World can muster. And this is factor which it is within our power to influence. […]

(3) All Soviet propaganda beyond Soviet security sphere is basically negative and destructive. It should therefore be relatively easy to combat it by any intelligent and really constructive program.

For those reasons I think we may approach calmly and with good heart [the] problem of how to deal with Russia. As to how this approach should be made, I only wish to advance, by way of conclusion, following comments: […]

(4) Much depends on health and vigor of our own society. World communism is like [a] malignant parasite which feeds only on diseased tissue. This is a point at which domestic and foreign policies need every courageous and incisive measure to solve internal problems of our own society, to improve self-confidence, discipline, morale and community spirit of our own people, is a diplomatic victory over Moscow worth a thousand diplomatic notes and joint communiqués. If we cannot abandon fatalism and indifference in face of deficiencies of our own society, Moscow will profit – Moscow cannot help profiting by them in its foreign policies.

(4) We must formulate and put forward for other nations a much more positive and constructive picture of [the] sort of world we would like to see than we have put forward in [the] past. It is not enough to urge people to develop political processes similar to our own. Many foreign peoples, in Europe at least, are tired and frightened by experiences of past, and are less interested in abstract freedom than in security. They are seeking guidance rather than responsibilities. We should be better able than Russians to give them this. And unless we do, Russians certainly will. […]

A concise, albeit anonymous, historical analysis of the telegram can be found here: http://www.articlemyriad.com/22.htm

M3 Zhdanov on the Founding of Cominform. September 1947

In September 1947 Communist party leaders from around the world gathered in Warsaw to form the Communist Information Bureau (Cominform). The excerpts below taken from Soviet leader Andrei Zhdanov's speech at the meeting provide a sample of the tough and uncompromising rhetoric that had by this time come to characterize Soviet views of US policy in Europe.

[…] the crusade against Communism proclaimed by America's ruling circle with the backing of the capitalist monopolies, leads as a logical consequence to the attacks on the fundamental rights and interests of the American working people [...] in poisoning the minds of the politically backward and unenlightened American masses with virus of chauvinism and militarism, and in stultifying the average American with the help of all the diverse means of anti-Soviet and anti-Communist propaganda – the cinema, the radio, the church and the press.

[...] The strategic plans of the United States envisage the creation in peacetime of numerous bases and vantage grounds situated at great distances from the American continent against the USSR and the countries of the new democracy. America has built, or is building, air and naval bases in Alaska, Japan, Italy, South Korea, China, Egypt, Iran, Turkey, Greece, Austria and Western Germany. There are American military missions in Afghanistan and even in Nepal. [...] Economic expansion is an important supplement to the realization of America's strategical plan. American imperialism is endeavoring [...] to take advantage of the post-war difficulties of the European countries, in particular the shortage of raw materials, fuel and food in the Allied countries that suffered most from the war, to dictate to them extortionate terms for any assistance rendered. [...] American economic 'assistance' pursues the broad aim of bringing Europe into bondage to American capital [...]

In their ideological struggle against the USSR, the American imperialists [...] demonstrate their ignorance by laying primary stress on the allegation that the Soviet Union is undemocratic and totalitarian, while the United States and Great Britain and the whole capitalist world are democratic [...]

One of the lines taken [...] is an attack on national sovereignty, an appeal for the renouncement of the sovereign rights of nations, to which is opposed the idea of a 'world government'. The purpose of this campaign to import the unbridled expansion of American imperialism, which is ruthlessly violating the sovereign rights of nations, to represent the United States as a champion of universal laws, and those who resist American penetration as believers in an obsolete and 'selfish' nationalism. The idea of 'world government' has been taken up by bourgeois intellectual cranks and pacifists [...] also as a slogan specially directed at the Soviet Union, which indefatigably and consistently upholds the principle of real equality and protection of the sovereign rights of all nations, big and small [...] Soviet foreign policy and, in particular, Soviet economic relations with foreign countries, are based on the principle of equality, on the principle that agreements must be of advantage to both parties [...] This fundamental feature of the agreements with the USSR with other states stands out particularly vividly just now, in the light of the unfair and unequal treaties concluded or planned by the United States. [...]

But the present position of the Communist Parties has its shortcomings. Some comrades understood the dissolution of the Comintern to imply the elimination of all ties, of all contact, between the fraternal Communist parties. But the experience has shown that such mutual isolation of the Communist Parties is wrong, harmful and, in point of fact, unnatural [...] The need for mutual consultation [...] has become particularly urgent at the present juncture when continued isolation may lead to a slackening of mutual understanding, and at times, even to serious blunders.

In view of the fact that the majority of the leaders of the Soviet parties (especially the British Labourites and the French Socialists) are acting as agents of the United States imperialist circles, there has developed upon the Communists the special historical task of leading the resistance to the American plan for the enthrallment of Europe, and of boldly denouncing all coadjutors of American imperialism in their own countries. [...] Just as in the past the Munich policy untied the hands of the Nazi aggressors, so today the concessions to the new course of the United States and the imperialist camp may encourage its inspirers to be even more insolent and aggressive [...]

Hanhimäki, Jussi: The Cold War, Oxford 2004, S. 50–52.

M4 Nuclear Fears / Nuclear Threats: Dulles on Massive Retaliation, 1954

In 1954 US Secretary of State John Foster Dulles (1888–1959) promised massive retaliation – meaning a full-scale nuclear attack – if the Soviet Bloc attacked any of America's allies.

The 'long time' factor is of critical importance. The Soviet Communists are planning for what they call 'an entire historical era,' and we should do the same. They seek, through many types of maneuvers, gradually to divide and weaken the free nations by overextending them in efforts which, as Lenin put it, are 'beyond their strength, so that they come to practical bankruptcy.' Then, said Lenin, 'our victory is assured. Then, said Stalin, will be 'the moment for the decisive blow.'

In the face of this strategy, measures cannot be judged adequate merely because they ward off an immediate danger. It is essential to do this, but it is also essential to do so without exhausting ourselves. [...]

We need allies and collective security. Our purpose is to make these relations more effective, less costly. This can be done by placing more reliance on deterrent power and less dependence on local defensive power.

This is accepted practice so far as local communities are concerned. We keep locks on our doors, but we do not have an armed guard in every home. We rely principally on a community security system so well equipped to punish any who break in and steal that, in fact, would-be aggressors are generally deterred. That is the modern way of getting maximum protection at a bearable cost.

What the Eisenhower administration seeks is a similar international security system. We want, for ourselves and the other free nations, a maximum deterrent at a bearable cost. [...]

Local defenses must be reinforced by the further deterrent of massive retaliatory power. A potential aggressor must know that he cannot always prescribe battle conditions

M5 Inside view of a private atomic bunker, USA 1950s

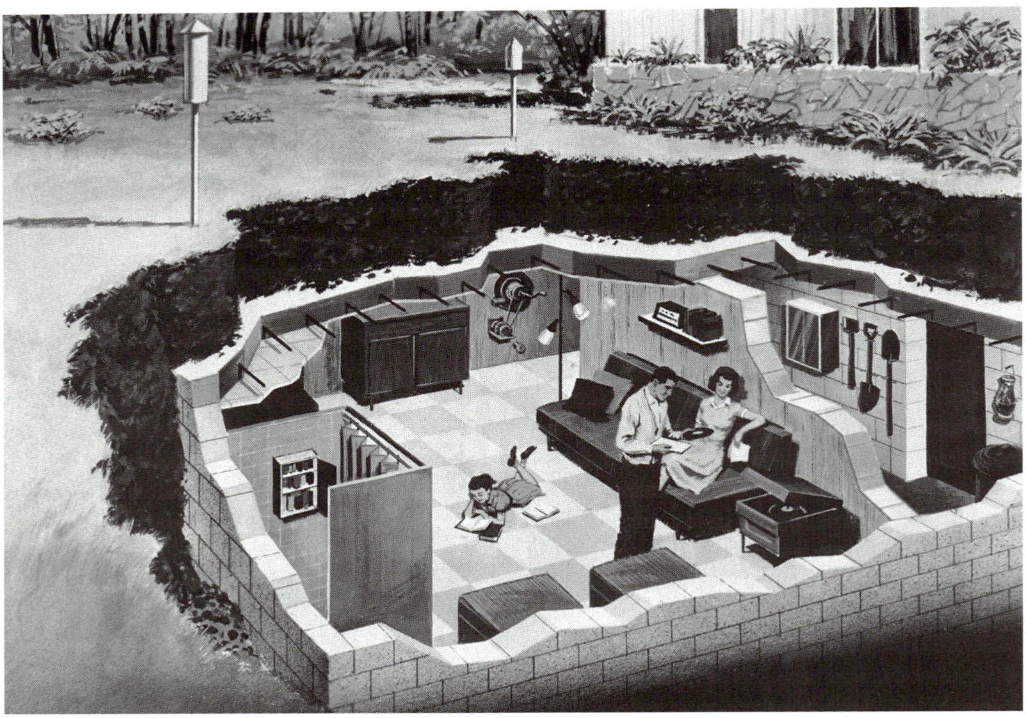

that suit him. Otherwise, for example, a potential aggressor, who is glutted with manpower, might be tempted to attack in confidence that resistance would be confined to manpower. He might be tempted to attack in places where his superiority was decisive.

The way to deter aggression is for the free community to be willing and able to respond vigorously at places and with means of its own choosing.

Hanhimäki, Jussi: The Cold War, Oxford 2004, S. 277–278.

M6 Nuclear War and its Consequences

The devastating results and inhumanity of (nuclear) mass-destruction can best be discussed when seen; there are a number of documentaries and movies which depict the horrors of nuclear warfare or the naive dealings with it in the USA. Best known (and easily available on DVD) are:

Documentary: Atomic Café (Jayne Loader/ Kevin Rafferty, USA, 1982; b/w + colour, 86 min.)
Animation/Drama: When the Wind Blows (Jimmy T. Murakami, UK, 1986; 80 min.)
Drama: The Day After (Nicholas Meyer, USA, 1983; 126 min.)

Recommendable are also some classics, although they may be inaccessible to some students, who are used to MTV-style TV and unable or unwilling to work with older films; still a good starting point for discussions and probably the closest one can get to the zeitgeist of the dawning atomic age:

Fictional Docu-Drama: The War Game (Peter Watkins, BBC, UK, 1965; b/w, 48 min.);
Comedy: Dr. Strangelove (Stanley Kubrick, UK, 1964; b/w, 96 min.)
Drama: Fail Safe (Sidney Lumet, USA, 1964; b/w, 112 min.)

5.2 Germany as Focal Point

M1 Ernest Bevin on the Significance of Germany, July 1948

The Berlin Blockade was seen by many as the gravest and most dangerous crisis in Europe since the end of World War II and as a significant test of the future of the Continent. In this excerpt, written at the start of the Blockade and the subsequent airlift, British foreign secretary Ernest Bevin presents an analysis of the significance of Germany to Prime Minister Clement Attlee.

1. A prosperous and contented Germany, built on sound democratic principles, is the best guarantee for the safety of Europe. These conditions cannot at present be secured in the Eastern Zone; it is therefore all the more important that they should be secured in the West. If our policy succeeds, Western Germany, forming part of the Western Defence System and contributing to the ERP [Economic Recovery Programme] can become a most effective barrier against the spread of Communism across Europe. On the other hand, if we fail, the only alternative is Soviet control on the whole of Germany and therefore Europe [...]

2. By far the greater part of Germany's industrial wealth and two thirds of the population are in the Western Zones. The Ruhr industries are essential to the success of the ER Programme. While economic conditions in the West are improving, the economy of the Eastern Zone has, as a result of wholesale removals by the Soviet, become desperate. Control of the West German economy and in particular a controlling interest in the Ruhr is therefore a major Soviet objective in Germany [...]

5. But our policy in Germany cannot be restricted to rehabilitating the Western Zones and allowing the Russians to evict us from Berlin. Berlin is regarded by the vast majority of Germans as the symbol of German unity and as the only possible capital for a united Germany. The mere fact of our continuing presence has so far prevented and shall continue to hinder the setting up in Berlin of a Soviet controlled German Government. At

the same time our struggle for position in the city has made it in the eyes of the Germans and of Europe generally a test case between the Soviet and the Western Powers in which prestige of both sides is heavily engaged. To retreat from Berlin, the last democratic island in the Soviet sphere, would immensely increase Soviet prestige, win over the doubtful masses in Germany to their side and depress our friends in each of the free countries in Europe. It would also encourage the Russians to hazard adventures in Vienna, Turkey or elsewhere. On the other hand, if we stand fast in Berlin we shall undoubtedly rally German opinion and gain the time which is so necessary to pursue the advantages we posses in the West.

6. We must however be clear in our minds that to stay in Berlin is a means to an end rather than an end in itself. In consequence it would be a mistake to buy a settlement in Berlin by concessions to the Russians which would give them influence in Eastern Germany and above all in the Ruhr. For their part the Russians are unlikely to make any concessions in Berlin unless they expect to obtain important advantages in Germany as a whole. We can therefore expect a progressive worsening of the position in Berlin as the winter approaches. It will indeed be difficult for us to meet all the Berliners' requirements from airborne attacks, but our policy should be to continue the air supply route to its maximum capacity. This may result in the Berliners going hungry and a complete standstill in industry resulting in unrest. The Russians are unlikely to agree to take on the responsibility of feeding the population of the Western sectors unless under conditions which are unacceptable to us. We should continue, however, to build up our air link to the maximum and maintain our garrison until the only alternative for the Soviet is to eject us by force. Meanwhile efforts should be made through the diplomatic channel to ascertain whether the Russians are prepared to negotiate a settlement on tolerable terms.

Hanhimäki, Jussi: The Cold War, Oxford 2004, S. 94–96.

M2 The Berlin Wall, 1961–1963

In August 1961, while the future of European integration was being debated, the East German government began the construction of the Berlin wall. Almost three years earlier, Soviet leader Nikita S. Khrushchev had provoked an international crisis by giving Western powers an ultimatum: negotiate a final settlement of the German question with the Soviets, or Moscow would sign a separate peace treaty with the German Democratic Republic, threatening Western occupation rights in (and access to) Berlin. While not so concerned over the West German military threat, Khrushchev had come under increasing pressure to stop the flow of talented East Germans to the West via Berlin, and had committed himself to the preservation of a socialist GDR. Thus the wall was essentially constructed to stop a potential disintegration of the East German state. In the first document-taken from a 3–5 August 1961 meeting of the Warsaw Pact leaders in Moscow – Khrushchev anticipates significant action on the Berlin – East German issue. Subsequent extracts are from the official exchange of notes between the United States and the Soviet Union a few days after the East German government began closing off the access routes between East and West Berlin. The last extract is from the most famous American statement on the Berlin Wall, issued by President John F. Kennedy during his visit to Berlin in June 1963.

A. Khrushchev, 4 August 1961

[…] We have to help the GDR out […] Everybody is guilty, and the GDR too. We let down our guard somewhat. Sixteen years passed and we did not alleviate pressures on the GDR […] What will it mean, if the GDR is liquidated? It will mean that the Bundeswehr will move to the Polish border, […] to the borders with Czechoslovakia, […] closer to our Soviet border […] If we level it [the GDR's living standard] down to our own, the result will be that the government and the party of the GDR will fall, consequently Adenauer will step in […]

You can imagine what satisfaction we'll get when we sign the peace treaty. Of course we're running a risk. But it is indispensable. Lenin took such a risk, when he said in 1917 that there was such a party that could seize power. Everybody just smirked and snorted then [...] World public opinion now is on our side not only in the neutral countries, but in America and in England. [...]

B. Exchange of Notes on the Berlin Wall, August 17 1961
United States Note

[...] The United States Government considers that the measures which the East German authorities have taken are illegal. It reiterates that it does not accept the pretension that the Soviet sector of Berlin forms a part of the so-called 'German Democratic Republic' and that Berlin is situated on its territory. Such a pretension is in itself a violation of the solemnly pledged word of the USSR in the Agreement on the Zones of Occupation in Germany and the administration of Greater Berlin. Moreover, the United States Government cannot admit the right of the East German authorities to authorize their armed forces to enter the Soviet sector of Berlin.
By the very admission of the East German authorities, the measures [...] are motivated by the fact that an ever increasing number of inhabitants of East Germany wish to leave this territory. The reasons for this exodus are known. They are simply the internal difficulties in East Germany. [...] The United States Government expects the Soviet Government to put an end to these illegal measures. This unilateral infringement of the quadripartite status of Berlin can only increase existing tension and dangers.

Soviet Reply

The Soviet Government fully understands and supports the actions of the Government of the German Democratic Republic [...] West Berlin has been transformed into a center of subversive activity diversion, and espionage, into a center of political and economic provocations against the G.D.R., the Soviet Union, and other socialist countries. Former and present West Berlin municipal leaders have cynically called West Berlin an 'arrow in the living body of the German Democratic Republic,' a 'front city,' a 'violator of tranquility,' the 'cheapest atom bomb put in the center of a socialist state.' [...]
The G.D.R. has displayed, over the course of many years, great tolerance in the face of such a completely disgraceful and impermissible situation. Implementing its consistently peace-loving and democratic policy, it has borne enormous sacrifices to facilitate the achievement of agreement between the two German states on the questions of peaceful settlement and reunification of Germany on peace-loving and democratic foundations [...] [M]easures taken by the Government of the G.D.R. are temporary. The Soviet Government repeatedly has emphasized that the conclusion of a peace treaty with Germany and normalization on such a basis of the situation in West Berlin will not infringe the interests of any of the parties and will contribute to the cause of peace and security of all peoples.

Hanhimäki, S. 328–331

C. Kennedy on the Significance of Berlin, June 1963

There are many people in the world who really don't understand, or say they don't, what is the great issue between the Free World and the Communist world. Let them come to Berlin. There are some who say that Communism is the wave of the future. Let them come to Berlin. And there are some who say in Europe and elsewhere we can work with the Communists. Let them come to Berlin. And there are even a few who say that it's true that Communism is an evil system, but it permits us to make economic progress. 'Laßt sie nach Berlin kommen.' Let them come to Berlin!
Freedom has many difficulties and democracy is not perfect, but we have never had to put a wall up to keep our people in, to prevent them from leaving us. I want to say, on behalf of my countrymen, who live many miles away on the other side of the Atlantic, who are far distant from you, that they take the greatest pride that they have been able to share with you, even from a distance, the story of the last

eighteen years. I know of no town, no city, that has been besieged for eighteen years that still lives with the vitality and the force and the hope and the determination of the city of West Berlin.

While the wall is the most obvious and vivid demonstration of the failures of the Communist system, for all the world to see, we take no satisfaction in it. For it is, as your Mayor has said, an offense not only against his town but an offense against humanity, separating families, dividing husbands and wives and brothers and sisters, and dividing a people who wish to be joined together.

What is true of this city is true of Germany, lasting peace in Europe can never be assured as long as one German out of four is denied the elementary right of free men, and that is to make a free choice. In eighteen years of peace and good faith, this generation of Germans has earned the right to be free, including the right to unite their families and their nation in lasting peace, with goodwill to all people. You live in a defended island of freedom, but your life is part of the main. So let me ask you, as I close, to lift your eyes beyond the dangers of today to the hopes of tomorrow, beyond the freedom merely of this city of Berlin, or your country of Germany, to the advance of freedom everywhere, beyond the wall to the day of peace with justice, beyond yourselves and ourselves to all mankind.

Freedom is indivisible, and when one man is enslaved, all are not free. When all are free, then we can look forward to that day when this city will be joined as one, and this country, and this great Continent of Europe, in a peaceful and hopeful globe. When that day finally comes, as it will, the people of West Berlin can take sober satisfaction in the fact that they were in the frontlines for almost two decades.

All free men, wherever they may live, are citizens of Berlin, and, therefore, as a free man, I take pride in the words ‚Ich bin ein Berliner.'

This famous speech is available as video and/or audio on the net, e.g.: http://www.americanrhetoric.com/speeches/jfkberliner.html

5.3 The End?

M1 The Reagan Challenge, 1982

Ronald Reagan took over as US president in 1981 and steered the country on a hard-right course – confrontational towards the Soviet Union and free-market oriented in domestic policies. Here is an excerpt from his speech to the British parliament in June 1982.

We're approaching the end of a bloody century plagued by a terrible political invention – totalitarianism. Optimism comes less easily today, not because democracy is less vigorous, but because democracy's enemies have refined their instruments of repression. Yet optimism is in order because day by day democracy is proving itself to be a not at all fragile flower. From Stettin on the Baltic to Vama on the Black Sea, the regimes planted by totalitarianism have had more than thirty years to establish their legitimacy. But none – not one regime – has yet been able to risk free elections. Regimes planted by bayonets do not take root.

The strength of the solidarity movement in Poland demonstrates the truth told in an underground joke in the Soviet Union. It is that the Soviet Union would remain a one-party nation even if an opposition party were permitted because everyone would join the opposition party. […]

Historians looking back at our time will note the consistent restraint and peaceful intentions of the West. They will note that it was the democracies who refused to use the threat of their nuclear monopoly in the forties and early fifties for territorial or imperial gain. Had that nuclear monopoly been in the hands of the Communist world, the map of Europe – indeed, the world – would look very different today. And certainly they will note it was not the democracies that invaded Afghanistan or suppressed Polish Solidarity or used chemical and toxin warfare in Afghanistan and Southeast Asia.

If history teaches anything, it teaches self-delusion in the face of unpleasant facts is folly. We see around us today the marks of our terrible dilemma – predictions of doomsday, antinuclear demonstrations, an arms race in which the West must, for its own protection, be an unwilling participant. At the same time we see totalitarian forces in the world who seek subversion and conflict around the globe to further their barbarous assault on the human spirit. What, then, is our course? Must civilization perish in a hail of fiery atoms? Must freedom wither in a quiet, deadening accommodation with totalitarian evil? […]

The hard evidence of totalitarian rule has caused in mankind an uprising of the intellect and will. Whether it is the growth of the new schools of economics in America or England or the appearance of the so-called new philosophers in France, there is one unifying thread running through the intellectual work of these groups – rejection of the arbitrary power of the state, the refusal to subordinate the rights of the individual to the superstate, the realization that collectivism stifles all the best human impulses […]

Chairman Brezhnev repeatedly has stressed that the competition of ideas and systems must continue and that this is entirely consistent with relaxation of tensions and peace. Well, we ask only that these systems begin by living up to their own constitutions, abiding by their own laws, and complying with the international obligations they have undertaken. We ask only for a process, a direction, a basic code of decency, not for an instant transformation. […]

While we must be cautious about forcing the pace of change, we must not hesitate to declare our ultimate objectives and to take concrete actions to move toward them. We must be staunch in our conviction that freedom is not the sole prerogative of a lucky few but the inalienable and universal right of all human beings. So states the United Nations Universal Declaration of Human Rights, which, among other things, guarantees free elections. […]

I've often wondered about the shyness of some of us in the West about standing for these ideals that have done so much to ease the plight of man and the hardships of our imperfect world. […]

Well, the emergency is upon us so let us be shy no longer. Let us go to our strength. Let us offer hope. Let us tell the world that a new age is not only possible but probable.

Hanhimäki, Jussi: The Cold War, Oxford 2004, S. 574–575.

5.4 From Foe to Friend?

It is interesting to follow the development of Ronald Reagan's assessments of the USSR. Starting from a very strict anti-Communist point of view, which he wasn't shy to convey in aggressive political rhetoric and the serious push for 'Star Wars', as his SDI-program was called by his critics, his later speeches showed understanding and even sympathy for 'the enemy'. This remarkable change can be traced in his speeches, key texts on the end of the Cold War, which lends itself to a small project or group work in which every group could analyze a different speech. The student's surprise that they are by the same author quickly bears fruit in a deeper understanding of political necessities and the drastic change in Cold War politics in the 1980s.

Reagan's so called Evil Empire Speech (1983): http://www.reagan.utexas.edu/archives/speeches/1983/30883b.htm; and his so called Ivan and Anya speech (1984): http://www.reagan.utexas.edu/archives/speeches/1984/11684a.htm

M1 Ronald Reagan and Mikhail Gorbachev on Human Rights, 1988

MEMORANDUM OF CONVERSATION

The President's First One-on-One Meeting With General Secretary Gorbachev

May 29, 1988, 3:26 p.m. – 4:37 p.m., St. Catherine Hall, The Kremlin, Moscow

[...] The President said that both sides had come a long way since he first wrote to Gorbachev in 1985. History would record the period positively, and that was true not just for our relations. [...] The President said he wished to digress for a minute and hand Gorbachev a list, as he had done on previous occasions. [...] The President continued that he would not go through the whole list; there were a dozen or so. But for some reason he felt a particularly affinity to one man on the list, Abe Stolar . He was an American, whose parents had come to America in the time of the czars. [...] When Stolar was young, he and his parents returned to Russia, and his son had eventually married a young lady in Russia. Now they had all decided they wanted to return to the land where Stolar was born, the United States, and the Soviet government gave permission to all but the daughter-in-law. So they all decided to stay behind until they could leave together. As Stolar put it, he wanted to die where he was born, and the President thought the Soviet authorities should allow the whole family to leave. [...]

Gorbachev responded that as always when the President presented specific humanitarian problems to him, especially concerning departures, these would be given careful attention. There was no obstacle to departure from the Soviet Union but one – possession of state secrets – and that was natural, since all countries wished to protect such secrets. But basically the Soviets did not keep people against their will.

Gorbachev went on to say that on the eve of his departure [...] the President had spoken about raising human rights in Moscow. [...] Gorbachev went on to say that the Soviets had many comments to make about the U.S. human rights situation; about problems of political rights, the rights of blacks and colored people, social and economic rights, the treatment of anti-war protesters and movements. They got many facts from the U.S. press. Probably they still did not know everything well. But they were ready to listen to what the U.S. side had to say. They were ready to have a conversation with the U.S. Congress. Gorbachev said he was calling for a seminar, on a continuous basis, involving officials, legislators and academics of the two sides, to discuss what was happening in the two countries. [...] The President said he knew what Gorbachev was saying. Some of it was true, as it was anyplace, because the U.S. was a big and varied country. It had many races, and one race, the blacks, had once been slaves. They were then freed, and discriminating against them was now illegal, but all the individual prejudices could not be immediately overcome. Some people in our country had brought them with them when they immigrated. But there was one difference: the U.S. had passed laws, and under the law no one could use prejudice to keep someone from getting a job, finding housing, getting an education, and the like. That would be against the law, and that person would be punished under the law, not because of his race or religion.

Gorbachev responded that there were many declarations and many provisions in the U.S. Constitution and U.S. laws. The problem was to look at how they were implemented in real life. If one looked at figures on unemployment of Blacks and Hispanics, on per capita income of Whites and Blacks, on access to education and health, there were big differences. In the Soviet Union, living standards were lower, even much lower than in the United States, but there was nothing like such large contrasts among groups of people in the country when it came to pay and the like.

The President responded that when slavery was lifted from the Blacks they started at a much lower level than others, and even the civil rights laws could not guarantee them equality when it came to jobs and schools, and the like. But when you considered that they had started lower, under the economic expansion of the past six years, wages and

employment among Blacks were rising faster than for Whites. In other words, they were catching up.
Gorbachev said he had not been inventing figures. He was citing facts from the American Congress. He did not want to teach lessons to the United States President on how to run America. He just wanted to note that the President had ideas about the Soviets, and the Soviets had ideas about the United States. Recently, the Soviets had become much more self-critical, but the U.S. had not. Once the Soviets had begun to be self-critical, it seemed that the U.S. spoke more about civil and ethical rights. [...]

http://www.margaretthatcher.org/archive/displaydocument.asp?docid=110610

The memorandums of the various summits, mainly Geneva and Reykjavik, provide many opportunities for working on 'original' source material. They can be downloaded as facsimile documents here: http://www.margaretthatcher.org/archive/us-reagan.asp; especially the second meeting on October 11, 1986 is noteworthy as here Reagan's notorious SDI-program and general arms reduction possibilities are discussed.

M2 The Soviet Union in Difficulties, May 1983

From the discussion at a meeting of the ruling Communist Party Politburo, 31 May 1983, headed by Juri Andropov.

[ANDROPOV.] Now I would like to address an issue, which in my opinion deserves an exchange of opinions and suggestions.
Today I've talked with a number of members of the Politburo about our government's announcement of the response to the deployment of American missiles 'Pershing-2' and cruise missiles in Western European countries; and also concerning the resolution adopted by the 'Big Seven' countries [G7] in Williamsburg. It's important that we discuss this matter, exchange opinions, and express suggestions that should be developed.
If you look at the events that are taking place in the Western countries, you can say that an anti-Soviet coalition is being formed out there. [...] The actions of President Reagan, the bearer and creator of all anti-Soviet ideas, creator of all untrue insinuations regarding our country and the other countries of the Socialist Community, deserve very critical and harsh reactions from our side. [...] The imperialist countries of the West want to put together a bloc against the USSR. They act together and, as you saw, Reagan managed, though with some pressure, to convince his partners in the 'Big Seven' to sign the resolution and express their opinions against the policies of the USSR [...] We have to open up a wider network to win public opinion, to mobilize public opinion in the Western countries of Europe and America against the deployment of nuclear weapons in Europe and against a new arms race, that is being forced [upon us] by the American administration. [...]
It is true that we shouldn't scare people with war. But in our propaganda we should show more clearly and fully the military actions of the Reagan administration and its supporters in Western Europe, which in other words means disclosing the full scale aggressive character of the enemy. We need that, so we could use facts to mobilize the Soviet people for the fulfillment of social and economic plans for development of the country. We can't, comrades, in this situation forget the defense needs of our country [...]
GORBACHEV. You said it right, Yuri Vladimirovich [Andropov], that the time now is calling us to increase our actions, taking the necessary steps to develop a broad program of counter-measures against the aggressive plans of the Western countries. And in our internal plan we have certain serious tasks. We can take some action towards the countries of CMEA [Council on Mutual Economic Assistance], the countries of the Warsaw Pact, and separate socialist countries. I completely support the suggestions about holding a meeting and other actions that were suggested here, including the military line. The United States is moving to Europe. Here we can't wait. We have to act [...]

Hanhimäki, Jussi: The Cold War, Oxford 2004, S. 576–578.

M3 Charles S. Maier: The Economic Collapse in East Germany

Many of the East European regimes attempted to borrow their way out of the economic difficulties of the 1980s. Among these was East Germany, in which the precarious state of the economy and the effects of indebtedness became increasingly visible to the leadership in the latter half of the decade. In this excerpt, historian Charles S. Maier (born 1939, currently Professor of History at Harvard University) portrays their increasing desperation.

[…] It was not foreordained that East German socialism had to collapse, but the financial pressures were becoming unrelenting. At the end, they culminated in a debt crisis, the extent of which astonished and demoralized party delegates. The GDR [German Democratic Republic], so Gerhard Schürer, head of the Planning Commission, reported to Honecker's successor, Egon Krenz, at the end of October 1989, had accumulated a foreign debt of 49 billion 'valuta marks' ($26.5 billion), the currency unit used for foreign trade accounting and pegged at roughly the value of the West German Deutsche Mark. The deficit on current account would amount to over $12 billion for 1989, and debt service alone cost $4.5 billion or over 60 percent of yearly export earnings. Just to stabilize the debt by an austerity program would require a drop in living standards of 25 to 30 percent, and even such a sacrifice could not assure that the GDR would be able to sell the needed exports. As in all national credit crises, the looming East German disaster had its origins in the persistent failures to resolve contending claims on national income. In this case the defects arose from ideological commitments. To understand the terminal crisis that overtook the regime, one has to work back to long-term disabilities imposed by socialist production. […]

Günter Ehrensperger dated the difficulties from November 1973, when Honecker responded to his projections that foreign debt would rise from its still modest 2 billion valuta marks total to 20 billion by 1980. "I was summoned to him on the same evening and he told me I was immediately to cease working on such calculations and studies. I was to receive no further material and I have to have all the statistical bases in the department destroyed. That was the beginning. […]" When Schürer confessed to the Central Committee the extent of foreign indebtedness, he claimed that the difficulties originated with the Eighth Party Congress in 1971, which resolved that German communism must support a generous consumer society and welfare state. Their decision enshrined what became known as 'the unity of social and economic policy,' which Günter Mittag stubbornly defended as party orthodoxy for the next decade and a half. In practice it meant subsidizing consumer prices, vacations, social services so that the gap with West Germany did not undermine the acceptance of the regime. But it also limited the investment that East Germany required to produce goods that might be internationally competitive. As Schürer told the Central Committee, "It was hardly visible then, but then was when the switches were set. From then on the train travelled millimeter by millimeter in the wrong direction. It travelled away from the realities of the GDR." […]

Hanhimäki, Jussi: The Cold War, Oxford 2004, S. 584–586.

M4 Robert Darnton: The Fall of the Berlin Wall, November 1989

After large demonstrations against the regime in many German cities, the new leaders of the East German Communist Party agreed to allow the people of East Berlin to visit across the Wall. But the East Berliners would not wait for an orderly transition. On 9 November tens of thousands forced their way to the Wall, and the border guards – demoralized and with no clear orders – let them through. Here is an excerpt from the American historian Robert Darnton`s (born 1939; currently Professor of European History at Princeton University) diary for that week in November.

On the morning after, November 10, when both Berlins woke up wondering whether the first look through the Wall had been a dream, the West Berlin tabloid *Volksblatt* ran two headlines, shoulder to shoulder, on its front page: 'The Wall is Gone' and 'Bonn Demands Destruction of the Wall.'

Both were right. The Wall is there and it is not there. On November 9, it cut through the heart of Berlin, a jagged wound in the middle of a great city, the Great Divide of the Cold War. On November 10, it had become a dance floor, a picture gallery, a bulletin board, a movie screen, a videocassette, a museum, and, as the woman who cleaned my office put it, 'nothing but a heap of stone.' The taking of the Wall, like the taking of the Bastille, transformed the world. No wonder that a day later, in Alexanderplatz, East Berlin, one conqueror of the Wall marched in a demonstration with a sign saying simply, '1789-1989.' He had helped dismantle the central symbol around which the postwar world had taken shape in the minds of millions.

To witness symbolic transformation on such a scale is a rare opportunity, and it raises many questions. To begin with the most concrete: What happened between November 9 and 12, and what does it mean?

The destruction of the Wall began in the early evening of Thursday, November 9, soon after the of East Berliners, or Ossis, as they are called by the West Berliners here, burst upon the West, [...] a young man with a knapsack on his back, somehow hoisted himself up on the Wall directly across from the Brandenburg Gate. He sauntered along the top of it, swinging his arms casually at his sides, a perfect target for the bullets that had felled many other wall jumpers, like Peter Fechter, an eighteen-year-old construction worker, who was shot and left to bleed to death a few feet in front of Checkpoint Charlie on August 17, 1962. Now, twenty-seven years later, a new generation of border guards took aim at a new kind of target and fired – but only with power hoses and without much conviction. [...] Of course, it is very difficult for a visitor from the West to know what people are really thinking in the East. But at a time of popular uprising, voices are raised and they can be heard. Few East Germans have clamoured for reunification with the Federal Republic, despite the blandishments of Chancellor Kohl. The East Germans probably want what they say they want in the banners they carry in their demonstrations. [...]

'Let the wall be painted on both sides.' We are the people, and we are millions.' 'No more wall in the head.' 'Travel, yes. Beg, no.' [...]

Hanhimäki, Jussi: The Cold War, Oxford 2004, S. 603–605.

M5 Mitterrand and Thatcher on German Unification, December 1989

Both French and British leaders were privately still suspicious of Germany and wanted to postpone unification between its two parts. Here are some statements by French president François Mitterrand and excerpts from his conversation with British Prime minister Margaret Thatcher at the end of 1989, excerpted from the diaries of Mitterrand's adviser Jacques Attali.

8 December 1989 [EU summit in Strasbourg; private conversation between the French President François Mitterrand and British Prime minister Margaret Thatcher]

T: The Four need to get together as soon as possible. In the GDR, people are increasingly calling for reunification. If that is what happens, it will present Gorbachev with a problem that he cannot control. This must be prevented by the actions of the CSCE [Conference on Security and Cooperation in Europe] and the Four Powers. The East Germans do not take the Four enough into consideration. They have forgotten that it is thanks to us that Berlin is free. Kohl has no idea of what feelings come up in Europe on hearing about reunification. Germany is divided because it was the Germans who have imposed the most terrible of wars on us so Germany becomes more dominant in Europe from one day to the next. It is necessary for us to meet regularly to create a counterweight to Germany. One has to make sure that she will not dominate, as Japan does. Douglas Hurd has spoken to Genscher about a meeting of the Four. He is very afraid that it will be about Berlin. Gorbachev must be very uneasy at the moment. If the crazy Germans attack the Soviet bases there will be terrible consequences.

M: When we spoke, Gorbachev was much tougher on Germany than he has been earlier. He recounted his conversation with Genscher. He talked about a German diktat. All of this must lead to excitement in the GDR where Soviet soldiers live with their families. The anger over the Germans has come back. But Gorbachev does not have any better means than we do; for psychological reasons, he can no longer use his divisions.

T: You are right. He can no longer, because of the recent developments in Poland. (She says this with a sense of regret.)

M: The Germans must think about this themselves if they are to move forward. The liberal party [FDP] has criticised Kohl's line, which is really easy to criticise. Willy Brandt has also expressed views close to ours. More reasonable forces are making themselves known in Germany. Kohl is speculating in the natural course of the German people, he wants to be the one who encourages it. Are there many Germans who will have enough character to resist these pressures? They have never found their borders, they have never had a destiny […] (The British Prime Minster opens her handbag and takes out two well-worn maps of Europe, cut out from a British magazine. The first one shows the European borders at the beginning of World War II, the second those that were drawn in Europe in 1945. She points to Silesia, Pomerania, East Prussia.) She says: They will take all of this, and Czechoslovakia.

M: Speeding up this process is really very dangerous.

T: Kohl will encourage it, he will inflame it! We have to place some limits on the Germans or that may really happen. They will make Berlin their capital again whatever happens.

M: Yes, and Gorbachev cannot prevent it any more than the United States [can].

T: The United States will not prevent it. There is a very strong pro-German lobby in America.

M: The American ambassador in Bonn, Vernon Walters, talks about reunification in five years. We do not have any means of power confronted with Germany. One is in the same situation as the French and British leaders before the war, who could not react to anything. We must not return to the situation at Munich! […]

T: First and foremost one must respect the borders. And then, when there has been fifteen years of democracy in the GDR, one may begin to talk of reunification.

M: We must create special relations between France and Great Britain just as in 1913 and 1938.

T: There are too many issues that come up at the same time! It is not just a German affair. If Germany controls events, she will get Eastern Europe in her power, just as Japan has done in the Pacific, and that will be unacceptable from our point of view. The others must join together to avoid it."

Hanhimäki, Jussi: The Cold War, Oxford 2004, S. 609–612.

5.5 Who won the Cold War?

M1 George Bush's State of the Union, 1992

Every January the President of the US addresses the public in his "State of The Union" to declare his political ideas and the program for the next year. In 1992 President George Bush recapitulates the end of the Cold War and declares a winner

Mr. Speaker, Mr. President, distinguished members of Congress, honored guests and fellow citizens:

I mean to speak tonight of big things, of big changes and the promises they hold and of some big problems and how together we can solve them and move our country forward as the undisputed leader of the age.

We gather tonight at a dramatic and deeply promising time in our history, and in the history of man on earth. For in the past 12 months, the world has known changes of almost biblical proportions. And even now, months after the failed coup that doomed a failed system, I am not sure we have absorbed the full impact, the full import of what happened.

But Communism died this year. Even as President, with the most fascinating possible vantage point, there were times when I was so busy helping to manage progress and lead change that I didn't always show the joy that was in my heart But the biggest thing that has happened in the world in my life, in our lives, is this: By the grace of God, America won the Cold War. And there's another to be singled out, though it may seem inelegant. I mean a mass of people called the American taxpayer. No ever thinks to thank the people who pay country's bill or an alliance's bill. But for a half Century now, the American people have shouldered the burden and paid taxes that were higher than they would have been to support a defense that was bigger than it would have been if Imperial Communism had never existed. But it did. But it doesn't anymore. And here is a fact I wouldn't mind the world acknowledging: The American taxpayer bore the brunt of the burden, and deserves a hunk of the glory.

And so, now, for the first time in 35 years, our strategic bombers stand down. No longer are they on round-the-clock alert. Tomorrow our children will go to school and study history and how plants grow. And they won't have, as my children did, air-raid drills in which they crawl under their desks and cover their heads in case of nuclear war. My grandchildren don't have to do that, and won't have the bad dreams children once had in decades past. There are still threats. But the long drawn-out dread is over. […]

Much good can come from the prudent use of power. And much good can come from this: A world once divided into two armed camps now recognizes one sole and pre-eminent power, the United States of America. And this they regard with no dread. For the world trusts us with power, and the world is right. They trust us to be fair, and restrained. They trust us to be on the side of decency. They trust us to do what's right. […]

Two years ago, I began planning cuts in military spending that reflected the changes of the new era. But now, this year, with Imperial Communism gone, that process can be accelerated. Tonight I can tell you of dramatic changes in our strategic nuclear force. These are actions we are taking on our own, because they are the right thing to do. […]

This weekend I will meet at Camp David with Boris Yeltsin of the Russian Federation. I have informed President Yeltsin that if the commonwealth, the former Soviet Union, will eliminate all land-based multiple-warhead ballistic missiles, I will do the following: We will eliminate all Peacekeeper missiles. We will reduce the number of warheads on Minuteman missiles to one and reduce the number of warheads on our sea-based missiles by about one-third. And we will convert a substantial portion of our strategic to primarily conventional use.

President Yeltsin's early response has been very positive, and I expect our talks at Camp David to be fruitful. I want you to know that for half a century, American presidents

have longed to make such decisions and say such words. But even in the midst of celebration, we must keep caution as a friend. For the world is still a dangerous place. Only the dead have seen the end of conflict. And though yesterday's challenges are behind us, tomorrow's are being born. [...]
And maybe for a moment it's good to remember what, in the dailyness of our lives, we forget. We are still and ever the freest nation on Earth, the kindest nation on Earth, the strongest nation on Earth. And we have always risen to the occasion. And we are going to lift this nation out of hard times inch by inch and day by day, and those who would stop us better step aside. Because I look at hard times and I make this vow: This will not stand. And so we move on, together, a rising nation, the once and future miracle that is still, this night, the hope of the world.

http://www.infoplease.com/t/hist/state-of-the-union/205.html

Literature

American Revolution:

Dudley, William (ed.) (1992): The American Revolution. Opposing Viewpoints. San Diego, Greenhaven Press.

Kurland, Philip B./Lerner, Ralph (ed.) (1987): The Founders' Constitution. Chigago, University of Chicago Press..

Industrialization:

Cipolla, Carlo (ed.) (1973): The Fontana Economic History of Europe, vol. 1–3, Fontana, Glasgow

Floud, Roderick/Johnson, Paul, eds. (2004): The Cambridge Economic History of Modern Britain, 2 vols., Cambridge University Press, Cambridge

Frader, Laura L. (2006): The Industrial Revolution, Oxford U.P., Oxford

Landes, David S. (1972; orig. 1969): The Unbound Prometheus, Cambridge U.P., Cambridge

Langton, John / Morris, R. J. (ed.) (2004, orig. 1986): Atlas of Industrializing Britain, Methuen, New York

Maddison, Angus (2006): The World Economy, OECD

Morgan, Kenneth (2004): The Birth of Industrial Britain, Pearson, Edinburgh

Overton, Mark (20044): Agricultural Revolution in England, Cambridge U. P.

Perry, Marvin, et al. (20035): Sources of the Western Tradition, Houghton Mifflin, Boston

Imperialism

Pakenham, Thomas (1991), The Scramble for Africa. 1876–1912. London, Weidefeld and Nicolson.

Smith, Bonnie G. (2000): Imperialism. A History in Documents. Oxfort.

Snyder, Luis L. (ed.) (1962), The Imperialism Reader. Documents and Reading on Modern Expansionism. Princeton.

Germany in Perspective:

Herwig, Holger (1997): The Outbreak of World War I, Houghton Mifflin, Boston/New York

Hite, John/Hinton, Chris(2000): Weimar and Nazi Germany, John Murray, London, p. 49;

Laver, John (1992): Imperial and Weimar Germany 1890–1933, Hodder & Stoughton, London

Layton, Geoff (20053): Weimar and the Rise of Nazi Germany 1918–33, Hodder Murray, London

Morris, Terry/Murphy, Derrick (2000): Europe 1870–1991, HarperCollins, London

Taylor, A. J. P. (1961): The Origins of the Second World War, Simon and Schuster, N. Y./London

Taylor, A. J. P. (2001; orig. 1945): The Course of German History, Routledge, London

Williamson, David (1994): War and Peace: International Relations 1914–45, Hodder & Stoughton, London

The Cold War

Hanhimäki, Jussi (ed.) (2004), The Cold War: a History in Documents and Eyewitness Accounts. Oxford, Oxford University Press.

Index